Date Due

OCT 15 1996		
OCT 1 6 1996		
TO:N		
SEP 2 6 1997	OCT 1 6 1997	
	AUG 1 1 2005	
OCT 3 1 1997		
NOV 1 3 1997 R	AUG 1 0 2005	
NOV 1 3 1997		
APR 0 1 1999		
APR 0 1 1999		
OCT 1 5 2007		
OCT 0 2 2007		
FEB 2 1 2008	FEB 1 5 2008	

CULTURES OF THE WORLD

SWEDEN

Delice Gan

MARSHALL CAVENDISH
New York • London • Sydney

Reference edition published 1993 by
Marshall Cavendish Corporation
2415 Jerusalem Avenue
P.O. Box 587
North Bellmore
New York 11710

Originated and designed by
Times Books International, an imprint of
Times Editions Pte Ltd

Printed in Singapore

Library of Congress Cataloging-in-Publication Data:
Fun, Delice Gan Cheng, 1954–
    Sweden / Delice Gan Cheng Fun.
      p. cm.—(Cultures Of The World)
    Includes bibliographical references and index.
    Summary: Introduces the geography, history,
    economy, culture, and people of the fourth
    largest country in Europe.
    ISBN 1-85435-452-3
    1. Sweden—Juvenile literature. [1. Sweden.]
I. Title. II. Series.
DL609.F76 1992
948.5—dc20   91–40377
                          CIP
                          AC

Cultures of the World

Editorial Director	Shirley Hew
Managing Editor	Shova Loh
Editors	Roseline Lum
	Goh Sui Noi
	June Khoo Ai Lin
	Siow Peng Han
	Leonard Lau
	Tan Kok Eng
	MaryLee Knowlton
Picture Editor	Yee May Kaung
Production	Edmund Lam
Design	Tuck Loong
	Ang Siew Lian
	Lee Woon Hong
	Lo Yen Yen
	Ong Su Ping
Illustrators	Suzana Fong
	Kelvin Sim
Cover Picture	Stefan Lindblom (Svenskt Pressfoto)

INTRODUCTION

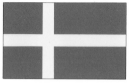

THE LAND OF THE MIDNIGHT SUN. Volvo cars. Tennis stars. Each of these, while stereotypical images, do represent different aspects of Sweden. They capture its beautiful unspoiled landscape, its efficiency and its belief in investing in the future. For a small nation of 8.5 million people, this northern European country has done very well.

As a country that in many ways has had a fair amount of luck, including good location and vast mineral resources, Sweden long ago did away with its military aggressiveness, settling instead to playing a balancing role among the world's many ideological and political sides. It is no coincidence that the world has often sought the help of Swedish politicians and leaders to fill the key positions of leadership in the United Nations and mediate conflicts that need to be solved.

But despite its high standard of living, welfare state and private enterprise, and its progressive social ideas, Sweden is undergoing changes that will alter its society for years to come.

As part of the series *Cultures of the World*, this book attempts to dispel the myths as well as tell the story behind the fleeting images we have of this country of the Vikings.

Stockholm

CONTENTS

"Even winter will not stop me from playing on this slide!" Swedish children gather in the neighborhood playground.

CONTENTS

Lovely flowers in a town square.

A neighborhood in the industrial city of Gothenburg.

GEOGRAPHY

SWEDEN IS THE FOURTH LARGEST COUNTRY IN EUROPE, with a surface area of 174,000 square miles. This makes it only slightly larger than the state of California. Located in the eastern part of the Scandinavian Peninsula, it has Norway to the west and the Gulf of Bothnia and the Baltic Sea to the east. To its far north and northeast is Finland.

It is one of the countries farthest from the equator, with the Arctic Circle crossing the northern part of the country. Situated at about the same latitude as Alaska, Sweden extends from north to south for a distance of about 1,000 miles. It is about 310 miles wide.

Opposite: **A pretty stream, with its source in the mountains in the background, flows down Tarfala Valley.**

Below: **Postcard-like scenes of snow can make Swedish winters very memorable.**

GEOLOGY

Sweden occupies a geologically stable part of the great Eurasian land mass. A land of ancient bedrock, it has a varied landscape of mountains, vast tracts of forests and plains. This is made even more interesting with lakes of all sizes dotting the countryside.

Mount Kebnekaise is, at 6,945 feet, the highest mountain in Sweden.

The southernmost part of the country is a continuation of the fertile plains of Denmark and northern Germany, while just above this, the terrain changes to heavily-wooded highlands with less rich soil. The rest of the south is broken up by hills, lakes and lowlands.

A borderline area separating the warmer south and the icy north is found just north of Stockholm, the capital. This vital area, full of rolling hills, forests and large river valleys, contains the country's oldest industrial region—Bergslagen, founded on rich deposits of iron and other ores.

Large iron ore deposits are also mined in the north, which led to the founding of the country's northernmost towns, Kiruna and Gällivare-Malmberget. Copper, lead and zinc ores are found in the region of Västerbotten, also in the northern part of the country.

A mountain range running north-south forms the backbone of the Scandinavian Peninsula, and also acts as a natural border between Sweden and Norway. The source of the country's largest rivers, such as the Angermanälven, is found in this range.

From the top of the Kaarevaara Mountains inside the Arctic Circle, one

can even see Norway and Finland. The highest point of this mountain range is only 1,696 feet, just a fraction of the country's highest peak, Kebnekaise, at 6,945 feet.

Sweden has been covered several times by inland ice, most recently during the last ice age which ended about 10,000 years ago. The landscape has changed due to the weight and movement of these massive glaciers; they have smoothed out mountains and rock formations, and created lakes and sandy ridges.

These ridges were used as travel paths in the lowlands, and later became important as sand pits. The fertile soil of the central Swedish plains today is a result of the finely ground material that was left behind after the glaciers disappeared. The land in central and northern Sweden has been rising, in some areas more than three feet, since the last ice age.

The beauty of Sweden comes alive with picturesque mountains and colorful forests.

COUNTRY OF 100,000 LAKES

Water continues to play a vital role in this nation. There are almost 100,000 lakes in Sweden, the largest being Lake Vänern. It is one of the largest in Europe, covering a total area of 2,156 square miles. Early industrial development first took place north of the lake, where the bedrock is rich in minerals.

Numerous rivers flow from the mountains in the northwest toward the Baltic Sea in the east. These waters have been harnessed to produce hydroelectric power, which plays an important part in the development of the country's industries. Hydroelectricity remains one of the major sources of energy while Swedish expertise and experience on this subject have been exported to other countries.

In the past, the rivers were used to transport logs for the forest industry. Sawmills and wood product factories were traditionally sited at the mouth of rivers in Norrland, the region that makes up northern Sweden.

THE LAND OF THE MIDNIGHT SUN

Sweden has relatively mild weather compared with other places of corresponding latitudes, such as Alaska or southern Greenland. This is due to the warm Gulf Stream in the Atlantic Ocean, as well as Sweden's location in the area between Arctic and warmer air masses.

The expression, "as changeable as the weather," is appreciated by the people as it can be rainy one day and sunny the next. As a result, the temperature differences between day and night, and summer and winter, are not so great in some areas. This is especially true of western Sweden.

There is, however, another type of weather which brings about a more contrasting climate. Stable, dry and sunny weather is brought by the high pressure zones in the east. It is this high pressure which leads to

hot spells in the summer and cold ones in the winter. In the summer, there is little difference in the weather between the north and south as the region of Norrland warms up due to the long days.

North of the Arctic Circle, the sun never sets in the months of June and July. The long summer days and equally long winter nights result from the tilt of the Earth's axis and its rotation around the sun. Even in Stockholm, summer nights can be bright with only a few hours of semi-darkness. This is why Sweden is called "The Land of the Midnight Sun."

The opposite is true in winter, where the ground is covered with snow from December to March. The sun sometimes goes into hiding for months, but there is usually some light around midday.

In the coastal areas in the south, the weather is milder. Here, inhabitants enjoy a longer fall and an earlier spring. For example, spring may arrive in the southern province of Skåne in February, while the northernmost part of Norrland may only see the end of winter in late May!

The sun appears on the horizon ... at midnight. The phenomenon of the midnight sun exists because the Earth's axis is tilted. During summer in the north, the North Pole leans toward the sun, thereby giving Sweden's north a period of continuous sunlight.

FLORA AND FAUNA

Swedes are very nature-conscious and children are taught from a very young age to respect and look after the environment. They have plenty of opportunities to come into contact with nature and learn about their surroundings as much of the country's landscape is wooded.

The forest is mainly made up of coniferous trees with a blending of deciduous trees, like birch and aspen, in the south. An interesting flora, including several types of orchids, can be found in parts of the Scandinavian mountain range and on the islands of Gotland and Oland, which have a lime-rich bedrock.

The fauna has been affected by both climate and history since the last ice age, and by human settlement. Bears and lynx roam the forests in the north, while large numbers of roe deer, moose, hare and fox are found throughout the country.

Moose, which are much sought after by hunters, often pose a traffic hazard when they cross roads between forests. It is common to see warning signs that say "Danger—Moose" on country roads.

Only a few species of birds remain in the winter, but in the warmer months, large numbers of migratory birds arrive from countries as far south as Egypt and South Africa.

In the countryside, where birds are protected, bird-lovers have a chance to spot species like the rare white-tailed eagle, the redshank and the wild swan.

The government has worked with the large forest industry to prevent deforestation. Today, there are more trees in the country than ever before.

There is a rich variety of water-borne life in this country of long coasts and many lakes. Environmental pollution, however, has taken its toll. One endangered species is the Baltic seal.

Fish is a popular food among the Swedes. They can choose from different varieties ranging from cod to mackerel from the deep, salty Atlantic, or salmon and pike which thrive in the less saline waters of the Gulf of Bothnia, and in lakes and rivers. Traditional food staples of the people include herring and Baltic herring, a smaller relative.

To protect the fauna, hunting and fishing are strictly regulated. Also, the government has set aside about 20 areas of natural beauty for preservation as national parks. In 1910, Sweden was the first nation in Europe to establish such parks.

Reindeer, reindeer everywhere! A woman helps to herd the animals into a farm.

CROWDED SOUTH, EMPTY NORTH

This country of 8.5 million people is divided into 24 counties. More than 85% of the population is concentrated in the south with its fertile lands and friendly climate. The most densely populated areas are within the triangle formed by the three largest urban centers, and along the Baltic coastline north of Stockholm.

The largest urban center, Greater Stockholm, includes the nation's capital and has a population of 1.4 million. Next is the Gothenburg area with about 700,000 inhabitants. The third is the Malmö urban center with slightly less than 500,000.

The population thins out toward the north. The interior of Norrland is so sparsely populated that providing adequate services and transportation facilities is a problem.

The island of Gamla Stan sits in the middle of canals and waterways in the older section of Stockholm.

STOCKHOLM

This beautiful capital city is surrounded by water—actually, it is made up of 14 islands, tracts of the mainland and several islets. It rests on two lakes: one half is on freshwater Lake Mälaren and the other is on Lake Saltsjön, which leads out to an archipelago and the Baltic Sea.

Freshwater and saltwater are separated by an island which holds the old city, Gamla Stan, and great artificial canals in the southern end. It is here at the old city that Stockholm was born before the 13th century.

The archipelago is one of Sweden's natural treasures. Made up of about 25,000 islands, it is used mainly for leisure activities in the summer. Most of the houses on these picturesque islands are summer homes. In spite of this, the whole area remains unspoiled.

But Stockholm is not just an attractive city and the seat of government, it is also the focal point of the country's economic activity. More than one-quarter of the labor force is found in Greater Stockholm, where about 20,000 companies are located. Together, these companies account for 25% of the country's total production.

Yet this city, home to the Swedish royal family, is far from being a crowded industrial center as the whole urban area is spread over some 2,500 square miles. And with typical Swedish concern for the environment, the waters around the city have been cleaned and filled with fish. It is not unusual to see anglers fishing for their dinner right in the heart of the city.

Stockholm, with its government buildings in the background, has been called one of the most beautiful cities in Europe.

15

HISTORY

THE FIRST SIGNS of human habitation in Sweden date back to about 10,000 years before the birth of Christ. Stone Age hunters came to this northern land mass as the ice which had covered this region began to retreat. From 8000 B.C. to 6000 B.C., early dwellers who hunted and fished for survival started to populate the country.

EARLY SWEDEN

Scientists have found stone tools that were in wide use during the Bronze Age, from 1800 B.C. to 500 B.C. Archeological excavations have unearthed bronze weapons and religious objects from this period, which was marked by a high level of culture reflected, for instance, in the artifacts found in graves.

The next period, the Iron Age, from 500 B.C. to A.D. 400, saw the beginnings of a more settled population when agriculture became the basis of the economy. The development of an agrarian society continued over the next two periods: that of the great migrations, from 400 to 500, and the Vendel period, from 550 to 800. The latter period got its name from the discovery of splendid boat graves at Vendel in the region of Uppland, where the Svea tribe settled. From this tribe came the name Sweden (or *Sverige*). In the 6th century, the warring Sveas began to exert their influence over their neighbors. A series of minor wars began, and by the beginning of the Viking Era in A.D. 800, the Sveas had expanded beyond their original seat of power at Lake Mälaren.

Above: **Rock carvings in the region of Tanum.**

Opposite: **The doorway to an ancient church on the isle of Gotland in the Baltic Sea.**

17

The law of the Viking was based on what was called "The Thing." This was an assembly to which the Viking king's power was subject. The king had to go to each Viking village in Sweden—which had its own "Thing" and leaders—to receive homage.

VIKINGS

The Vikings were fierce plunderers who directed their expansion toward many parts of Europe. Their raids were first recorded in the late 8th century with an attack on a rich abbey at Lindisfarne on the northeastern coast of England. They were described as barbarians who killed monks and burned books.

These fearsome people were excellent sailors who had developed a superior shipbuilding technology. Their longships had the advantage of being strong enough to sail in stormy seas, while the shallow draughts allowed them to beach for surprise attacks on settlements.

However, the era was not only a period of plundering but also of trade. The Swedish Vikings' expeditions mainly traveled east along the coasts of the Baltic Sea, and down major rivers which went deep into present-day Soviet Union.

Along these waterways, they set up trading stations and short-lived principalities, like that of Rurik at Novgorod. They also went as far as the Black and Caspian seas, where they formed trading links with the Byzantine Empire and the Arab dominions. Some of these Vikings even remained in Byzantium as members of an elite imperial guard.

Around the 10th century, the Vikings founded the city of Kiev as a result of a profitable trade in furs, honey and amber. At the same time, these travelers brought home precious metals like gold and silver, and luxury goods like cloth. These and other artifacts, such as coins from Arabia, have been found at the site of Sweden's first city, Birka. This early trading center was on the island of Björkö on Lake Mälaren, where its fertile valley gave rise to the first center of power in Sweden. Today, the nation's capital also lies on this important lake.

The expansion eastward continued into the 12th and 13th centuries with the absorption of present-day Finland after several expeditions.

The Vikings left behind many wonderful myths which were told originally by poets who spun them through their imagination. The myths covered the creation of humanity as well as the exploits of Viking gods such as Odin, the leader of the gods, and his warrior maids, the Valkyrs (or Valkyries).

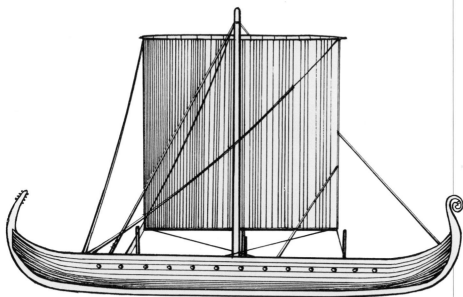

The Viking longship, truly a masterpiece in terms of shipbuilding. This exceptionally sea-worthy ship is designed to enable the craft to take tremendous pounding in rough seas.

EARLY CHRISTIANITY

Christianity came soon after the Vikings drew attention, through their expeditions, to their northern homeland. Christianity arrived in the 9th century through Ansgar, a Benedictine monk. He succeeded in converting some of the inhabitants.

But in spite of his efforts and those of others, pagan beliefs continued to persist. The old Viking religion, with its gods like Thor (god of thunder), Frey (god of fertility) and Odin, continued to be practiced by some well into the following century. Customs varied from one region to another. Some even involved human sacrifices.

It was only in the later part of the 11th century that Sweden truly became Christianized. When King Erik Jedvarsson converted to Christianity in the mid-12th century, paganism was no longer practiced. The king was later canonized as St. Erik and became the patron saint of Sweden.

MAKING OF A KINGDOM

At about the same time, King Erik and his family were involved in a struggle for power with the Sverker family. The crown went back and forth between the two families from 1160 to 1250. But the monarchy was still not the central authority, even though the various provinces had become a single unit around the year 1000. Each province retained its own assembly and laws.

A kingdom of Sweden started to come into being in 1280, when King Magnus Ladulås established a temporal nobility and introduced a form of European feudalism. A council with representatives from the nobility and the church was also set up to advise the king.

This new order, to some extent, went against the old Viking idea of the chief as the first among equals. The farmers, however, held on to their rights and privileges and prevented the implementation of a full feudal system. These ancient rights, which had been handed down orally and were written down during this period, formed Europe's oldest body of written law. Centuries before, the Vikings had brought the rights of the ordinary person to England.

By the middle of the 14th century, Sweden became a kingdom when a law code for the whole country was established during the reign of King Magnus Eriksson.

HANSA PERIOD

Trade flourished in the 14th century, especially with the German towns, under the leadership of Lübeck in the Hansa period. The next 200 years, when trade was dominated by the Hanseatic League, was a vital period in Sweden's history.

The vigorous commercial activity led to the founding of numerous towns in Sweden. Germanic influence was not confined to commerce but spread also to the political, social and cultural spheres. Even the language assimilated many linguistic forms from the German spoken by the Hanseatic traders. Contact with the Hansa drew Sweden into the circle of culture on the European continent.

In spite of the enhanced trading activity, agriculture remained the basis of the economy and was developed through improved methods and tools. But the economy went into decline in the late 14th century when the Black Death arrived. This resulted in a reduced population and many abandoned farms.

It was not until the second half of the 15th century that the crisis was overcome. At this time, iron production began to play an increasingly significant role in the economy.

The Black Death, the great bubonic and pneumonic plague that ravaged Europe between 1347 and 1351, originated in Asia and quickly overtook Europe, including Scandinavia in 1350. About one-third of Sweden's population died.

UNION OF KALMAR

Meanwhile, the Union of Kalmar, from 1397 to 1521, was formed under Queen Margaret of Denmark. It involved an agreement that Denmark, Norway and Sweden should have one and the same monarchy. Earlier, in 1389, the crowns of these Scandinavian countries had already been united under the Danish queen as a result of inheritance and family ties.

But this period, dominated by Denmark as it was the most advanced of the Scandinavian countries, was marked by conflict rather than unity. The conflicts were between the central government, represented by the monarchy, and the high nobility, together with the sometimes rebellious burghers and peasants. Enmeshed with these clashes were efforts to preserve Sweden's national unity and its economic interests.

In 1434, a revolt against the Danish king, Erik of Pomerania, was led by Sweden's first great national hero, Engelbrekt Engelbrektsson. He played a major, but brief, political role until he was murdered by the son of one of his enemies. King Erik was deposed but the struggle went on between powerful families who were either for or against the union.

The final turning point came in 1471 when Sten Sture, a man of ordinary birth, led the Swedes in the Battle of Brunkeburg against the Danes. The Swedes won decisively, but the union continued for another 50 years. Still, this victory and Sture's subsequent role as statesman prevented Sweden from being completely reintegrated into the union.

By this time, the first steps toward parliamentary government had been taken. A national assembly with representatives of the four estates—nobles, clergymen, burghers and peasants—was set up. But Swedish nationalism and renewed ties with the Hansa, as well as struggles for power between the state and the church, led to further Danish attacks.

These conflicts culminated in the "Bloodbath of Stockholm" in 1520 when the Danish union king, Kristian II, ordered the execution of more than 80 leading men in Sweden. This terrible act eventually led to his downfall in the rebellion which followed. The leader of the rebellion, Swedish nobleman Gustav Eriksson Vasa, whose father and other relatives were killed in the Bloodbath, was subsequently crowned king of Sweden in 1523.

GUSTAV VASA

The reign of Gustav Vasa, from 1523 to 1560, is a highlight in the history of the country as the foundations of Sweden as a national state were laid. First, the new king turned the church into a national institution and took the property of the Roman Catholic Church. These actions, including the introduction of the Protestant Reformation, laid the ground for the Lutheran state religion.

Gustav Vasa also reorganized the administration along German lines and concentrated power in the hands of the king. He went on to strengthen the crown by declaring the monarchy hereditary in 1544. Previously, the king was elected, which meant that the aristocracy could assert itself each time the throne was vacant.

In that same year, he also reformed the parliament and planned a form of national military service. It made Sweden the first European country to have an army in peacetime.

There was no doubt that this reformer ruled firmly, concentrating power in his hands and curbing some liberties. Nonetheless, he is remembered as the king who gave the country a sense of nationhood.

A GREAT POWER

After Gustav Vasa's death, his sons struggled against each other for the throne. As a consequence, his eldest son, Erik XIV, ruled from 1560 to 1568. Then his second son, Johan II, took over the throne from 1568 to 1592, and Johan's son, Sigismund, from 1592 to 1599. Gustav Vasa's youngest son, Karl IX, then ruled from 1599 to 1611. But in spite of the infighting, Sweden prospered. The University of Uppsala, founded in 1477, flourished and immigration was encouraged.

Sweden enjoyed military successes under the reign of Gustav II, son of Karl IX. During his rule, from 1611 to 1632, the kingdom expanded to include a part of the Baltic states and Poland. He also made his country more powerful than Denmark for the first time. Known as Gustavus Adolphus abroad, he became involved in the Thirty Years' War on the side of the German Protestants in 1630. He had by then become a leading monarch in Europe and was recognized as a military genius.

After his death on the battlefield in Lützen in 1632, Sweden continued to expand. It defeated Denmark in two wars which resulted in the addition of some Danish and Norwegian provinces to its kingdom. All of these remain part of Sweden today. More territorial expansions were made under Axel Oxenstierna, who became temporary regent as Gustav II's daughter, Kristina, was too young to assume the throne. Later, the growth of the country's power continued during her reign. But she is better remembered for the major scandal she caused when she abdicated in 1654, and converted from the Protestant faith to Roman Catholicism.

Her cousin, Karl X, succeeded her to the throne and maintained the country's expansionist policy. Under his reign, Sweden reached the apex of its geographical size and political importance. By 1658, after a pact, known as the Peace of Roskilde, was made with Denmark, Sweden

While Gustav Adolf was away at war most of the time, Axel Oxenstierna ran Sweden smoothly. He helped establish a new Supreme Court, reorganized the national assembly, extended the university at Uppsala, and fostered mining and other industries that provided the bulk of the country's wealth.

became a great power in northern Europe. The kingdom included Finland, a number of provinces in northern Germany and the Baltic republic of present-day Estonia. For a while, it even had a colony in what is now the state of Delaware in the United States.

Karl XI ascended the throne after the death of Karl X in 1660. Unlike his predecessors, he turned his attention homeward and gave the people two decades of peace. He introduced several political reforms but also strengthened the position of the crown. He reduced the power of the nobility, which had gained strength during the wartime years when huge areas of land were given to them in exchange for supporting the monarchy. The nobles were made to surrender a large part of these lands to the crown and to the farmers.

But this peace was not to continue, for when Karl XII came to the throne at the end of the 17th century, Sweden became embroiled in hostilities again. Karl XII was the country's last warrior king, a romantic figure thought to be a military genius second only to Gustav II. However, under his rule, from 1696 to 1718, most of the earlier conquests were lost. His defeat in the Great Northern War, which lasted 21 years, against the armies of Denmark, Poland and Russia reduced the country's borders to largely those of Sweden and Finland today.

Finland was lost to Russia during the Napoleonic Wars in the early 19th century, and even the last possessions in northern Germany were ceded. But as compensation for these losses, the elected heir to the throne, the French marshal Jean Baptiste Bernadotte, managed to obtain Norway. It was forced into a union with Sweden in 1814, until that was dissolved peacefully in 1905.

Since the union with Norway, Sweden has not been involved in any other war, remaining neutral in times of conflict.

Gustav III was a popular king. He started hospitals, granted freedom of worship and removed many state controls over the economy. Unfortunately, he was assassinated at a dance in the Stockholm Opera House by some members of the Swedish aristocracy, who were angry with him for siding with the commoners on too many issues.

ERA OF LIBERTY

The country underwent major changes in the 18th century. The Swedish parliament, tired of royal autocracy, managed to introduce a new constitution after the death of Karl XII in 1718. In the new constitution, power was taken away from the monarchy and given to parliament. Parliamentary government was developed during this period, from 1719 to 1772, called the Era of Liberty. During this time, the party dominant in parliament formed the government, which in turn was responsible to the parliamentary body.

This age was dominated politically by two groups: the Hats, who were mercantile nobles, and the Caps, who were liberal commoners and urban traders. It was also during this period that trade began to take on more importance, although the economy remained basically agrarian until well into the 19th century. The government also encouraged iron and copper mining. Different hand-made goods soon found their way to Europe and beyond through trading organizations such as the Swedish East India Company.

It was altogether an era of growth, economically, culturally and scientifically. Parliament passed a Freedom of the Press Act in 1766, making Sweden one of the first countries to protect the liberties of the press. It still provides the basis of legislation for the media today.

The final years of this period saw the power struggles in parliament polarize the nobility and the non-privileged classes. The reigning king, Gustav III, took advantage of the situation and reduced the power of the parliament through a bloodless coup in 1772. This marked the end of the rule of the four estates and the reintroduction of absolute rule, even though enlightened.

Although the king's domestic policies were rather successful, he is

The narrow cobblestone streets of Gamla Stan, the oldest part of the city of Stockholm, bear testimony to the capital's ancient past.

remembered as a patron of the fine arts. During his rule, culture was encouraged and developed. He was responsible for the building of the Stockholm Dramatic Theater and the magnificent Royal Opera House. He also founded several academies for different areas of the fine arts, most notably the Swedish Academy of Literature, which is today well known for awarding the Nobel Prize for literature.

NEW BALANCE

In the early 19th century Sweden faced an economic crisis brought about by the Napoleonic Wars. There was widespread unhappiness under the rule of Gustav IV Adolf, who lacked the abilities of his father, Gustav III, who was assassinated. Finland was lost to Russia and the king was deposed in a bloodless revolt by the military and nobility. His uncle, Karl XIII, was elected.

A new constitution was adopted which struck a power balance between the monarchy and parliament. This was the start of the democratic monarchy. Parliament elected Jean Baptiste Bernadotte, a French marshal who was close to Napoleon Bonaparte, to be heir to the throne in 1810. When he was crowned in 1818, he had already been in power for a number of years. His conservative policies won him the support of the old ruling class. Nonetheless, a liberal opposition began to form during his reign.

The entrance to the Parliament House.

The reigns of his sons, Oscar I and Karl XV, saw liberal ideas become reality. These included the setting up of compulsory education and elementary schools, the abolition of the guild system, and the implementation of free trade. Perhaps the most vital changes politically were the introduction of local self-government and the reform of parliament. This resulted in a bicameral system which survived until 1971 with the introduction of a unicameral (one chamber) parliament.

Rail transportation developed in the second half of the 19th century and opened up forest industries, like lumbering. But even with these changes, Sweden remained a poor country with 90% of its population dependent on agriculture. As a result of this poverty, many emigrated, mainly to North America, between 1866 and 1914. More than 1 million Swedes, about one-fifth of the population, left for greener pastures.

The 19th century also saw the growth of strong popular movements like the temperance and women's movements, the free churches, the co-operative movement and, most importantly, the labor movement. The last movement grew in tandem with industrialization, which took place in the last part of the century.

The Riksdagshuset or Swedish Parliament House looks like the Roman Coliseum from the side.

SOCIAL DEMOCRATS

The turn of the century saw Sweden transformed into a modern industrial state. Universal suffrage for men was introduced in 1909, and for women in 1912. It was among the first countries to give women the right to vote.

The foundations of a welfare society were laid in the 1930s when the Social Democratic Party came into power. The party has dominated the government since 1932 and has held power for most of the last half century. However, it was dealt a severe blow when voters abandoned it for other parties in the 1991 election. It was their worst defeat in six decades, and many people doubt if it will ever recover from this blow.

GOVERNMENT

THE CONSTITUTION, which consists of three documents, contains the principles of government and provides the rights and freedom of the people.

THE CONSTITUTION

The most important document is the Instrument of Government which contains the basic rules of government and society. It states that all public power in Sweden comes from the people. It also states that democracy is based on "freedom of opinion and on universal and equal suffrage."

This document defines the different types of rights and freedoms. Among the absolute rights, which cannot be restricted unless through a constitutional amendment, are the freedom to worship, protection from being forced to make known one's political and religious views, protection of citizenship and the prohibition of capital punishment.

Among those rights which may be restricted by the law are freedom of speech, freedom of association and protection from the restraint of liberty. However, the constitution also covers how far these restrictions may extend.

The second document is the Act of Succession, which regulates the succession to the throne, while the third document, the Freedom of Press Act, provides the right to publish without restrictions and allows citizens access to all public papers.

Above: **The House of the Nobility.**

Opposite: **The beautiful City Hall in Stockholm.**

The 1986 assassination of Prime Minister Olof Palme stunned the country like no other event in recent Swedish politics. It served to shatter the illusion Swedes had of their country being a safe and non-violent place.

THE PARLIAMENT

Parliament, which has 349 members, is the main representative of the people. Members from different political parties are elected every three years. Swedes who are 18 and above have the right to vote, and voter turn-out is usually high, at about 90%.

Elections are by proportional representation. This means that the seats in parliament are distributed among the parties in proportion to the number of votes that they get. A qualification to this rule is that a party must gain at least 4% of the national vote to gain a seat.

The Swedish parliament has only one chamber. It is presided over by the speaker of parliament who is responsible for proposing the prime minister for parliamentary approval. The prime minister in turn appoints other ministers to the cabinet.

Basically, political power lies with the cabinet and the party or parties to which ministers belong. The cabinet is made up of 21 ministers, who have to give up their right to vote in parliament if they join the cabinet. Official substitutes take their places.

The work of parliament is carried out by 16 standing committees, each dealing with a different area such as the constitution, finance and budgeting, and other concerns covered by the ministries. It is the job of parliament to approve national taxes, annual budgets and legislation. The standing committees are required to study bills which are proposed by the government and members of parliament (MPs), and subsequently make their reports at a plenary session, which is when all MPs and the cabinet meet.

Sweden has an interesting blend of political and social ideas. It is a democracy with a welfare policy which has retained a vestige of its past by continuing to have a monarchy.

THE MONARCHY

Sweden has a constitutional monarchy. The constitution of the country defines the role of the king as the head of state. But his function is largely a ceremonial one, and he performs several official duties, like the opening of parliament each October. The king has no political power and plays no role in politics.

The present king is Carl XIV, a descendant of the Bernadotte family. The king, who came to the throne in 1973, acts as the official representative of his country. His consort is the German-born Queen Silvia. He will be succeeded eventually by his daughter, who is the first of three children. The Act of Succession was amended in 1979 to give males and females equal rights to the throne. The heir to the throne is the first-born.

POLITICAL PARTIES

In the early 18th century, Swedish political parties, known as the Hats and the Caps, tried to strengthen the power of the people in parliament. However, the governing authorities kept most, if not all, of the power.

After World War I, the authorities gave in to expanded voting rights and different political parties began to gain prominence. The Social Democratic Party soon became the largest and most powerful. After strikes and labor unrest hit the country during the 1920s and 1930s, the Social Democrats came into power.

The new government had some radical objectives, known as "the middle way." This form of government soon gained Sweden a reputation for industrial progress and peace. The popularity of this middle ground approach allowed the Social Democratic Party to hold power for most of the last 60 years.

Five parties were elected to parliament in 1921 when universal suffrage was introduced for the first time. In recent elections the Christian Democratic Party, the New Democracy Party and the Green Party of Sweden were also voted in.

Besides the Social Democrats and the above three, parties that have been in parliament before include the Left Party Communists, the Moderate Party, the Liberal Party and the Center Party.

Until recently, politics had been a question of balance between two party blocks, the socialists (the Social Democrats and the Left Party Communists) and the non-socialists (the Moderates, Liberals, Centrists and Christians). Coalition governments were formed among the Center, Moderate and Liberal parties in various alliances. When the Social Democrats were briefly out of power from 1976 to 1982, a Liberal Party minority government took over.

Going into the 1990s, Sweden faces a tremendous transition: it has to integrate and adjust its social welfare system and taxes as well as its attitudes and perceptions toward being a part of a new Europe. At the same time, the country has to tackle its serious economic problems caused by many years of low productivity and high wage claims.

In the 1991 election, the Social Democrats suffered their worst election defeat in more than 60 years, with voters blaming them for bad conditions in the country.

Sweden was swamped with huge financial problems, high taxes and inflation and an oversized public sector, a dramatic increase in crime, and a stagnant economy. Then there was the powerful social welfare system that had run out of control. This made many Swedes unhappy because, in order to finance the vast welfare program, they had to pay some of the highest taxes in the Western world.

As a result, the country had the highest inflation and lowest growth rates in Europe. This resulted in droves of Swedes casting their votes for the non-socialist parties on the central-right: the Moderates, Liberals, Centrists and Christians.

A couple rowing a boat in the calm waters in front of the parliament building.

Parliament in session in
the Riksdag.

LOCAL GOVERNMENT

The local government provides certain basic services and facilities, and
these tasks are run by municipalities. There are 284 municipalities run by
councils elected by the people.

One of the councils' biggest and most important tasks is providing
quality education in the many elementary, intermediate and high schools
in the country. They also provide child and old-age care, public health
and environmental hygiene, electricity and gas, street cleaning and garbage
collection. To carry out these services, the councils levy a tax and charge
fees. However, they also receive large federal subsidies for the services
which they have to provide according to law.

Between this level and the national government is the regional unit.
There are 24 counties at this level and their chief responsibility is providing
medical care. Aside from a few government-run and private hospitals,
the county councils own all hospitals in Sweden. The training of nurses
and other health-care professionals is also their responsibility. Counties
are entitled to levy an income tax to cover their expenses.

THE OMBUDSMAN

The position of the ombudsman (om-boodz-mahn), a Swedish concept, was set up primarily to provide some kind of check on the work of public agencies. Besides monitoring these agencies, the ombudsman also looks into complaints from the public against incorrect or unfair treatment. This idea has spread to other countries and institutions with the aim of protecting the individual.

The oldest form of ombudsman is the office of the parliamentary ombudsman, which dates from 1809. It was formed to give parliament a safeguard over how laws were used by judges, civil servants and military officers. Today, there are four parliamentary ombudsmen who cover all national and municipal agencies. But they cannot investigate cabinet ministers, members of parliament and municipal council members.

About 3,000 complaints are received annually by these ombudsmen, who will investigate and choose either to mediate or take legal action against the offending party.

Other government-appointed ombudsmen include the competition ombudsman, whose job is to ensure fair business practices based on the law, and the consumer ombudsman, whose work is like what Ralph Nader does in the United States, in that he or she tries to ensure that consumers are protected against misleading advertising, unsafe products and improper business practices like unreasonable contracts.

The press ombudsman is not appointed by the government but has been established by three national press organizations: the National Press Club, the Union of Journalists and the Newspaper Publishers Association. These ombudsmen examine complaints by people who think that certain newspaper stories have violated press ethics and wish to be protected against the invasion of their privacy.

The office of the equal opportunities ombudsman was set up in 1980 to ensure that the law concerning sexual equality at work is observed. Besides handling individual cases of discrimination in the workplace and in society, these ombudsmen also help to shape public opinion and recommend ways, including legislation, to fight unequal treatment.

Swedes young and old wave the flag and cheer.

A NEUTRAL COUNTRY

Sweden has adopted a policy of neutrality, which means that it does not align itself with any political or military alliance during peacetime, and remains neutral in times of war. Therefore, the country has not sought membership in alliances such as the North Atlantic Treaty Organization. For this reason, the country has worked to ensure self-sufficiency in areas necessary for its survival in times of conflict, such as agriculture, textiles and defense.

However, because of dramatic changes in the international scene recently—such as the changes in government in East European countries—Sweden is re-examining the idea of neutrality. It is still too early to say where this rethinking might lead. Some indication can be seen in the country's application to join the European Community. A few years ago, this would have been unthinkable.

THE SWEDISH FLAG

June 6, National Day, was originally celebrated as Swedish Flag Day. This date was chosen because it was the day on which Gustav Vasa, who laid the foundation of the Swedish state, was elected king in 1523.

It was also the day in 1809 on which the country adopted a new constitution which enshrined civil rights and liberties.

There are 15 official flag days, including the special celebrations of the royal family, May Day, Election Day and Nobel Day. It is not known when the flag, a yellow cross on a dark blue background, was first used. It is thought that the design came from the Danish flag and the colors from the Swedish coat of arms.

THE NATIONAL COAT OF ARMS

There are two Swedish National Coat of Arms: the Lesser Coat of Arms and the Greater Coat of Arms. The Lesser Coat of Arms is blue in color, with three crowns of gold and a closed crown sitting atop the shield. This crown on top is sometimes encircled with the chain of the Order of the Seraphim, which is Sweden's most distinguished order.

The triple crown design can be traced back to 1336 as the emblem of Sweden. It was then a symbol of the Three Wise Kings. The Lesser Coat of Arms is used more frequently than the Greater Coat of Arms, which belongs to the monarch.

The Greater Coat of Arms, the arrangement of which dates from the 15th century, is used only on special occasions by the government and parliament.

The shield is divided into four parts and contains the triple crown device and the "Folkunga Lion," which was the arms of the ruling house from 1250 to 1364. In the center are the arms of the present ruling house, the Bernadottes.

These arms represent the Vasa Dynasty and the bridge representing the Italian principality of Ponte Corvo, a gift to Jean Baptiste Bernadotte from Napoleon Bonaparte in 1809. The arms are complemented by the Napoleonic eagle and seven stars.

THE NATIONAL ANTHEM

Called *Du gamla, du fria* (Thou ancient, thou freeborn), the national anthem was written by a ballad writer, Richard Dybeck, in the 19th century and set to a folk melody from the province of Västmanland. It was sung frequently at the turn of the century and later became the national anthem.

ECONOMY

POLITICIANS AND ECONOMISTS have frequently spoken about "the Swedish model," a concept which came about in the late 1930s. It refers to the way in which Sweden fostered prosperity while seemingly avoiding the pitfalls of both communism and capitalism.

THE SWEDISH MODEL

Many countries have studied how Sweden's socialist government has steered "the middle way." This model, however, appears to have run out of solutions for the 1990s and the average Swede has run out of patience with it. Still, the "middle way" can be considered to have been a success over the last 50 years. A key factor for this is the cooperation and collaboration of the three main players in the economy: government, labor and business. Unlike other socialist nations, the Swedish government has not tried to nationalize key industries.

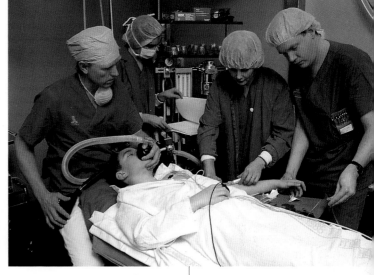

Above: **A patient undergoing surgery. Sweden's health programs and services are some of the best in Europe.**

Opposite: **Anna Karin Hansson, a typical blue-collar worker at the Volvo assembly line.**

The economy is a mixed one: there are private and public enterprises, with essential sectors such as the telecommunications network, postal service, energy production and other infrastructure owned by the state.

The public sector is also responsible for social services like health care, education and social welfare. It is one of the largest employers in the country, with one in three people working in the public sector at some level. The other big employer is the business sector, about 90% of which is privately owned. The remaining 10% is in the hands of cooperative societies and the state.

MAJOR INDUSTRIAL SECTORS

These sectors in Sweden began only about 100 years ago. The early industrial companies drew upon Sweden's rich natural resources and depended on materials like wood and metal ores. Many of today's new industries, which have replaced the old ones in importance, owe their success to the pioneer industries.

Modern Swedish companies are characterized by their specialized products, use of high technology, and emphasis on research and development.

Industry is dominated by a few large companies, some of which are multi-nationals. More than 40% of the industrial work force are employed by the country's 20 largest companies.

A Swedish airliner about to take to the skies. Swedish aircraft engineering is so advanced that they have built their own jet fighters—like the *Saab Viggen*, one of the best in the world—to protect the country.

ENGINEERING

This industry is both the largest and fastest growing in Sweden. It employs some 10% of the total labor force of 4.5 million. It is made up of five main sectors: manufacture of metal products, transportation equipment and instruments, mechanical engineering, and electrical engineering.

The engineering industry is found mainly in the urban areas of Stockholm, Gothenburg and Malmö. Made up of small- and medium-sized companies, this industry is highly dependent on trade and exports about half of its output.

Among the exports are some famous Swedish inventions and

innovations: ball bearings, automatic lighthouses, cream separators and telephones.

The most important subsector in engineering is the automotive industry, which exports about 75% of its products. There are two major manufacturers: Volvo and Saab-Scania. Volvo, which produces cars, trucks, buses, heavy engines and aircraft components, is Sweden's largest enterprise.

Electrical engineering and electronics form another vital sector where high technology is developed and used. Products include telecommunications systems, computers and industrial robots. The ratio of robots to workers used in Sweden is among the highest in the world.

Workers at the Saab-Scania automobile plant in Södertälje installing an engine.

Swedish economist Gunnar Myrdal once noted that Swedes have not only been lucky in terms of their economy, they have also made use of their luck. Their neutrality policy and leadership in United Nations peacekeeping activities have made them many friends; and through this, they have developed close economic ties with many nations.

CHEMICALS

The chemical industry grew faster than most other big domestic industries during the period after World War II. Growth sectors include organic chemicals, plastics and pharmaceuticals. The pharmaceutical sector, one of the biggest chemical products groups, exports as much as 80–90% of its output. It spends more money on research and development than any other industrial sector. Research projects include genetic engineering, drugs for heart disease, and eye surgery.

Biotechnology and its industrial uses, based mainly on knowledge from medical research, was another source of expansion in the 1980s. Swedish expertise in this area includes plant breeding, waste water treatment, metal extraction and processes for making plastic and other chemicals. More recently, petrochemicals, a branch of organic chemistry, has been an engine of growth for the whole chemical industry.

Chemical production, usually part of an industrial group whose main interests are in metal production or the pulp industry, is mainly in the hands of some 50 companies. Usually of moderate size, these companies are found in a few industrial regions in the south and the north, where the pulp and paper mills provide by-products and a ready market.

One of Sweden's most well-known researchers in this industry is Alfred Nobel, who lived in the 19th century. He was the inventor of dynamite but is better known for establishing the Nobel Prize, given annually to those who have excelled in their field of work.

IRON AND STEEL

The iron and steel industries were the sparks which set off industrialization at the turn of the century. Today's flourishing engineering industry is a

result of the domestic manufacture of iron and non-ferrous metal goods. Although mining has now declined in importance, Sweden remains the sixth largest iron ore exporter in the world. About 90% comes from the great ore fields at Kiruna and Malmberget in Lapland. Large amounts of copper, lead, zinc, silver and gold are also mined in the north.

Sweden is one of the world's biggest importers of steel because of its engineering industry. The steel industry specializes in producing high-grade iron and steel. Products such as ball bearings, razor blades, watch and valve springs are made. About one-third of ordinary steel products are used in various industries, construction and shipbuilding.

Swedish icebreakers come in all shapes, sizes and colors. This ice-breaker brightens up the docks with its rainbow colors.

CONSTRUCTION

The boom in the construction industry came in the 1960s and 1970s due to urban migration, increased demands for better housing standards and easier financing for building projects.

Internationally, Swedish construction companies have done well, helping to build infrastructure projects such as dams, harbors, railways and power stations in many countries. Their chief exports are technical knowledge and project management. Currently, their largest foreign markets are the Middle East and Africa. Export projects are a vital factor in the long-term growth of this industry, which employs almost 20% of the total labor force.

STATE-OWNED SECTOR

Since the oil crisis of 1973, the government has taken measures to help floundering industries like shipbuilding, steel, textiles and forestry by taking a major ownership role.

This sector includes seven public service enterprises which are responsible for the national railways, postal service and telecommunications systems among others. The state also owns a few companies such as Fortia AB, a holding company which has several firms in its fold in different industries like tobacco, foodstuff, chemicals and textiles.

AGRICULTURE

Less than 10% of Sweden's land is arable. Most of the cultivated land and arable farms are privately owned and work is carried out mainly by families. Only 3% of the work force is engaged in this activity. Although resources devoted to agriculture are small, it is nonetheless a vital activity.

There is a great variation of conditions between the north, where the smallest farms are found, and the south, where many different types of crops are grown. In the south, crops include wheat, sugar beet, potatoes, oil seeds and peas for canning. In central Sweden, cereals, fodder grain and plants that yield oil are cultivated. In the north, where the growing season is shorter, forage and seed potatoes are grown.

Most of the harvest provides feed for livestock which adds up to about 75% of agricultural earnings. Beef and dairy cattle, pigs, sheep and poultry are among the livestock on the farms, which are highly mechanized. Reindeer is bred in the north by the Samis.

Above: **Green, fertile plains in the region of Skåne help to establish self-sufficiency for the Swedes.**

Opposite top: **The giant hydroelectric power station at Laxede.**

Opposite bottom: **The skill of weaving. Today, weaving is not so much an industry as an art form in Sweden.**

A forklift hauling wood
for export.

FORESTRY

The forestry industry is important economically to this country, where
more than half the land area is forested. It employs 175,000 people and
is, in many regions, the principal economic activity. Most of Sweden's
forests, which represent just under 1% of the world's dense forests,
occupy the northern temperate coniferous belt. The rest, temperate mixed
forests, are found in the south. The main types of trees include Norway
spruce, Scots pine, birch, aspen, oak and beech. The success of the
industry has not resulted in deforestation but, instead, acreage has grown.
Companies are careful not to destroy the environment but to regenerate
the forests. Public bodies and companies each own about a quarter of the
forest area, while the rest is in private hands.

The industry produces paper and paper board, pulp, sawn timber and other products. It is dominated by large companies which have their own forests, transportation facilities and manufacturing plants. The lumbering industry is the largest in Western Europe and produces about 3.5% of the world output and 11% of world exports. The main importers of Swedish wood are Great Britain, Germany, Denmark and the Netherlands.

THE COOPERATIVE MOVEMENT

This movement offers an alternative between private and public ownership of companies. It constitutes the "third power" in the economy. A cooperative is a type of company which is organized by and for a group of people who want their interests met in different roles, for example, as a consumer, producer and resident. Members of a cooperative have a say in the running of the company, which is not tied to any political or religious organization.

Some facts provide an idea of how important such companies are to the country. It is estimated that two out of three people have some link with the movement; cooperative stores account for some 20% of sales of daily goods; and the KF Group, the national body of consumer cooperatives, is one of the country's largest enterprises.

There are six major cooperative organizations which cover a wide range of activities, from housing to burials. These are: the Swedish Cooperative Union and Wholesale Society—also known as the KF Group—the federal body for 138 consumer cooperative societies with a total of 2 million members; two housing cooperative organizations, HSB and Riksbyggen, which together account for one-third of the annual housing production; Folksam, a trade union/ cooperative insurance company which covers more than half of the population; OK Petroleum AB, a result of a merger between the oil consumers' cooperative body and the state-owned petroleum company, which has about a 20% share of the gasoline market; and the National Federation of Burial Societies (FONUS), which is the country's largest funeral company. FONUS also helps in other related matters such as tax and insurance questions.

A giant crane on a floating dock unloading goods from a cargo ship.

FOREIGN TRADE

Sweden depends heavily on trade. It needs to export a great deal of what it produces, and at the same time, import to meet domestic demands. Export of goods and services accounts for about one-third of the gross national product. The main goods for export are engineering (which make up the largest group) and chemical products, raw materials such as petroleum and iron ore, paper and paperboard, iron and steel and, increasingly, decorative glass and furniture. Also on the increase is the export of health care systems and forestry products.

A large part of its imports consists of industrial input goods, which are either finished in Sweden or used as components. The major imports include motor vehicles, power plants and business machines, foodstuff, raw materials, chemical products, input goods, and consumer and investment goods.

Most of Sweden's trade is with Germany, Great Britain, the United States, Norway, Denmark and Finland. The United States is its third largest customer as well as supplier; exports include steel, paper and paperboard, scientific instruments, consumer goods and automobiles—which account for 30% of all exports.

TRADE UNIONS

Sweden is known for its relatively stable work force. There is a high rate—more than 53%—of the population working. Also, the rate of women workers is among the highest in Europe.

The importance of trade unions in Sweden is reflected in the high unionization rate—more than three-quarters of all eligible employees are members. There are three national bodies under which the unions group: the Swedish Trade Union Conference (LO) for blue-collar unions, which brings together more than 90% of the workers; the Central Organization of Salaried Employees (TCO), which covers 75% of white-collar employees; and the Confederation of Professional Associations (SACO/SR), also for white-collar workers.

A huge oil platform under construction at Gothenburg harbor.

Sweden had a system of centralized wage bargaining until recently. This was because a framework on wages and working conditions was worked out between the LO and the SAF, the main employers' federation. Today, negotiations on such matters take place only at the level of the individual industry.

SWEDES

TODAY, IT IS A MISCONCEPTION to think of all Swedes as tall, blonde and blue-eyed. Since the 1940s, the country has accepted immigrants from many parts of the world. One million Swedes out of a population of 8.5 million are immigrants or have one immigrant parent.

DEMOGRAPHY

Most Swedes are descendants of the Germanic tribes that came to Scandinavia thousands of years ago. The first complete population census taken in 1749 showed that there were 1.8 million people. The demographic pattern of Sweden is the same as that of other industrialized countries, where high mortality and fertility rates were followed by lows on both counts as the country progressed and prospered.

The average density of population today is only 53 people per square mile, but this figure is misleading since the majority of the population live in the southern part of the country. Thus the density varies from 231 people per square mile in Stockholm county to three in Norrbotton, the northernmost county.

About 83% of the population live in urban communities, with the cities being the main places of growth. Most of the population growth, which took place between 1950 and 1970, occurred in three main areas: around Lake Mälaren with Stockholm as the center; on the west coast around Gothenburg; and in the south around Malmö. Today, about half the population of Sweden live in these areas.

Above: **Sweden no longer consists of only blonde and blue-eyed people; today, Swedes represent many races and nationalities.**

Opposite: **A Swedish girl posing in her national dress.**

EMIGRATION TRENDS

Mass emigration took place between the 1850s and the 1930s. About 80% of the emigrants went to North America while the rest settled in other Nordic countries.

Two Swedes braving the cold for a walk.

Poverty, the lack of work, increased information about other lands, plus a growing population contributed to social unrest in the 19th century.

This situation was made worse by failed harvests and famine which eventually sparked off the first wave of mass emigration between 1853 and 1873.

About 3% of the population—103,000 people—resettled in the United States, especially in the Midwest states of Minnesota, Nebraska and Wisconsin.

Emigration picked up again in 1879 after a combination of an economic slump in Sweden and boom years in the United States. On the average, about 34,000 Swedes emigrated annually to North America until 1893. By 1900, the Swedish economy had declined to a level lower than that of Norway, considered the junior partner in the Scandinavian group.

All told, almost 1.4 million people left between 1865 and 1930. Many stayed for good in their new homelands but about 25% later returned to Sweden.

FAMILY STRUCTURE AND PLANNING

A family enjoying an outdoor meal in the summer.

The nuclear family is the most important social unit in Sweden.

At present, Sweden has one of the highest fertility rates in Europe, with a birth rate of 1.96 per couple. This is partly because women born in the 1950s and 1960s delayed having children until now. This phenomenon, a result of women's increased involvement in education and work, has pushed up the average age at which women have their first child.

However, the marriage rate has fallen as the number of unmarried people living together has increased over the last 20 years. Along with France, Sweden may have the lowest marriage rate in the industrialized world. One couple in five live together or cohabitate; some do this for a period of time before they get married. And in 1987, as many as half of all babies were born out of wedlock.

Sami herders capturing a reindeer.

THE SAMI

The Samis, who live in the arctic region, have been in Sweden since the pre-Christian age. It is believed that they came in nomadic groups from the east at various periods of time and traveled through southern Finland to eventually settle in the interior of the Finnish-Scandinavian land mass.

Today, some 40,000–50,000 Samis are found all over the entire Finnish-Scandinavian arctic region and along the mountains on both sides of the Swedish-Norwegian border. About 15,000–17,000 live in Sweden and vary in their commitment to their culture. Some identify strongly with being a separate ethnic group while others have been assimilated into Swedish culture.

Sami children can go to a regular state-supported school or a state-run nomad school. Both types have the same aims except the nomad schools include teaching the Sami language and culture. Those who choose to go to a regular school can still learn their language and culture at home through a special home language project. Efforts are being made to preserve and renew the language of this minority group, especially since it does not have a strong written tradition. The culture has been passed down orally, and takes the form of *yoiking*, a kind of singing.

Reindeer breeding, once dominant, now no longer holds the same significance. Only some 2,500 people are engaged in the breeding of the animals for their meat. Previously, they were bred for milk and used as beasts of burden. The importance of reindeer breeding can be seen in the way breeders are still organized. They belong to a village which is an administrative and economic unit as well as a geographic grazing area. Common facilities are planned, constructed and maintained by the village and the costs shared among its inhabitants.

Over the years, nomadism has ceased as the breeders and their families have established permanent settlements in the low fell region, where the mountain reindeer mate and have their calves. Today, only the herders follow the animals; and in keeping with modern times, they use aircraft, motor vehicles and snow scooters to do their job.

Reindeer breeding, however, is not very profitable as it requires at least a herd of 500 to earn enough to support a family. Also, the 1986 nuclear accident at Chernobyl in the USSR has had a lasting impact on the reindeer, and it will be many years before the meat will be free of caesium and fit for consumption.

Thus, many families supplement their income through other means such as hunting, fishing, handicrafts and tourism. The last two are most evident at the winter market fairs at Jokkmokk. Genuine Sami handicraft made from traditional materials are found here, as well as delicacies like *lappkok*, a broth of reindeer marrow bones and shredded liver.

There are three dialects in the Sami language which belong to the Finno-Ugric group: Central or North Sami, the most widely spoken, is used in northern Sweden and Norway, and the far north of Finland; South Sami is the dialect of those in north-central Sweden and central Norway; East Sami is spoken in eastern Finland, from Lake Inari to the Kola Peninsula in the Soviet Union.

Swedes of all ages gather in a Stockholm park where the main attraction is a giant chess set.

THE CHANGING FACE OF THE SWEDE

SINCE THE SECOND WORLD WAR Immigrants have played an increasingly important role in Sweden since the end of the Second World War. They have accounted for almost 45% of the population increase from 1944 to 1980. During the war, this neutral country welcomed many refugees from other Nordic nations and the Baltic states. Many from neighboring countries returned home when the war ended. But at the same time, there was a jump in demand for workers which led to a great inflow of foreigners.

Many came from Finland, Norway and Denmark when an agreement was signed in 1954 creating a common labor market among these countries.

THE PRESENT ERA The ethnic and cultural mix became more apparent in the 1960s when the country experienced two big wavws of immigration due to its growing industrialization.

The first, in the mid-1960s, saw the arrival of workers from Yugoslavia, Greece and Turkey. The second took place between 1968 and 1970, with most coming from Finland.

Junior takes a ride on a sled, with a little help and support from Mom.

As the economy slowed down in the 1970s, so did the inflow of foreign workers. Since then, there have been few arrivals from the Nordic countries. Now, the reason for immigration has changed from economics to politics. The bulk of immigrants today consist of political refugees and their families. They come from such different cultures and climates as Chile, Iran, Iraq, Ethiopia and Turkey.

Recognizing the ethnic diversity of the immigrants, the authorities have come up with a number of measures to help integrate newcomers into Swedish society.

These are based on a policy which aims to establish equality between immigrants and Swedes, freedom of cultural choice and cooperation, and solidarity between the Swedish majority and the various ethnic minorities.

Swedish parents prefer that their children play with puzzles and other intellectually stimulating toys.

IMMIGRANTS Toward these ends, some 30 national immigration organizations have been set up, through government grants, to give minority groups a collective voice. Immigrants have a newspaper, printed in 12 different languages, to keep them informed of events in Sweden. But more important are the language programs that include courses in Swedish, paid by the government, for newly-arrived adults. There are also home language programs which enable immigrant children to receive instruction in their native language. This is part of the effort to help preserve ethnic cultures and languages.

Also significant is the right of foreigners, who have lived in Sweden for at least three years, to vote and run for office in local and regional elections. Non-Swedish citizens also have the same rights as Swedes with regard to social benefits and education.

FOLK DRESS

There are more than 400 types of folk costumes in use today. Originally worn by peasants, these are used nowadays for festive occasions or as formal attire. They are no longer worn for the same functions or with the same significance as before.

Each costume represents a particular rural district and is recognizable through the type of fabric used, the embroidery, and the accessories, among other things. Not all folk costumes today are exact replicas of those worn in the centuries before, as many of these local or regional dresses have been redesigned.

There is, however, a national folk costume for women which was put together by painter Gustaf Ankarcrona and artist Carl Larsson in the 19th century. The costume consists of a blue skirt with a yellow apron and a red bodice which are embroided with white daisies.

There are strict rules as to how to wear a folk dress as well as what to wear. It was important to wear it correctly, but practices can vary greatly from region to region. For example, in some places, unmarried girls can go bare-headed while in others they have to braid their hair and bind it with a red band or wear an open-ended bonnet.

Married women must always have their heads covered, quite often by a white linen bonnet, although today the stiff frame cap is preferred. Married women are also expected to tie up their hair with white ribbons. The headgear also indicates whether the wearer is going to a festive or sad occasion. Men's folk dress is not as colorful as the women's. Most of the costumes include knee breeches, a shirt and a vest. Again, the headgear reveals the status of the wearer—only men wear hats, and the hat band or braid tells if they are married or not.

LIFESTYLE

THE WAY OF LIFE for the average Swede is to a large extent defined by the welfare state. Working people pay high income taxes, one of the highest rates in the world. These high taxes and the high cost of living usually mean that few families can survive on one income, and both partners in a family must go out to work.

THE STATE PROVIDES

All basic social and medical services are provided by the state. Those using these services, which range from the district doctor to daily child care, pay a small fee, often according to how much they earn. These services also include education which is available to everyone, regardless of wealth. There are few private schools and universities. All young people have a chance to go to college or university through a state loan, which is repaid after graduation and upon getting a job.

Even then, the large amount of money people have to pay has taken a heavy toll. Swedish voters have shifted their support away from the ruling party that had shaped the welfare system that provided cradle-to-grave services in return for soaring taxes. The welfare state—which many Swedes consider suffocating and exerting too much influence—may well be going out of style.

Opposite: **While traveling to their favorite vacation spots, many Swedes love to stop by restaurants— such as this windmill cum café—for some rest and refreshments.**

Below: **Children on an excursion in Angerman-land, on the island of Ulvön.**

LIVING TOGETHER

A current word in the Swedish language is *sambo*, which refers to the person that one is living with. To all intents and purposes, the *sambo* is the husband or wife except that the couple is not married. Cohabitation, living together without being married, is common in Sweden. Many partnerships are said to be unmarried. And many of these couples have children.

Marriage, however, has not gone out of style. Nowadays, many postpone it to a later date when both partners are more settled in their jobs. Frequently, children attend their parents' wedding. At the same time, the separation rate is high, with about half of all marriages ending in divorce. The divorce rate is one of the highest in the Western world. And there is an increase in single-parent families.

CHILDREN AND CHILDCARE

The daily routine of most families begins with the children being dropped off at a daycare center or school before the parents go to work. For most young children, spending the day in a center during the work week is a way of life. When they grow older, the day is divided between school and the care center.

Sweden's highly developed system of childcare centers has allowed women to work outside the home. At the same time, the high cost of living and high taxes also mean that both partners must work so that the family can live comfortably.

Several benefits, however, are available to employees so that they can combine work with having a family. Many young couples make use of the generous period of paid leave—not found in many other countries—

when they have a child. Either parent can have a total of 15 months away from work. Sometimes this leave is shared between the mother and father. While fathers have not made use of this benefit as much as mothers, it is quite common, nonetheless, to see men pushing strollers down the mall in the middle of a working day. This paid leave can also be delayed and spread over eight years.

Swedes in general are a people who love children, and they have ensured that children's rights are protected. Children have their own ombudsman who looks after their interests. Also, parents are forbidden by law to hit their children.

Namnsdag, or names day, is almost as important as one's birthday in Sweden. Each day of the year has been given a name, for example July 23 is Emma and December 11 is Daniel. Thus, everyone (with a Swedish name, that is) will have a day for his or her name and this is marked by greeting cards or flowers from family and friends. It is not celebrated the same way as a birthday, but it is a day that will not go unnoticed.

Two Swedes laze by a small river for a picnic that includes free breathtaking scenery.

SOCIAL INTERACTION

The climate plays a role in social interaction in this long northern country. The pattern of work and play is related to short winter days that are bitterly cold, and the warm summer days with long daylight hours. This is especially true the farther north one goes.

As the gloom and cold set in toward the end of the year, many Swedes huddle down to an unvarying routine of commuting between work and home. As temperatures fall, the streets of cities and towns quickly empty by 7 p.m., long after the sun has set in many parts of the country.

The Swedish character seems more introverted and less sociable at this time of the year. There is little social interaction outside of the office and family. It is not surprising then that Swedes make such a fuss about celebrating Christmas, which is an opportunity to break an otherwise tedious winter.

As spring arrives—and the day lengthens—the transformation in Swedes is marked. When the days lengthen, so does the patience. When the thawing of the country begins, the inhabitants, too, seem to thaw. Faces that were moody in the long, cold winter months finally relax when the sun comes up. Social talk that involved only the casual short greeting now blossoms into prolonged chatter. Everywhere, laughter is heard. The unsociability gives way to conviviality, and outdoor cafés spring up like mushrooms, filled with people intent on making up for the long inactive winter.

During the warmer months, the streets teem with life while the people, seemingly less stressed, make the rounds of summer barbecues and picnics. It is a cycle that repeats itself every year. It is less evident in the southern part of the country, where winter is not as cold and the days are not as short.

Relaxing by the sea and having a drink is the best way to spend a lazy Swedish day.

EQUALITY AND WOMEN

Modern Sweden is a society with few class differences. Today, it is difficult to notice any between the working class and the middle class. This has been due partly to the narrow income gap between skilled and unskilled workers, and to the tax system which further closed the gap. At the same time, the country's fast economic growth in the 1960s brought a uniformly high standard of living.

Ulrika Hydman, one of the country's leading glass designers.

Attention has now turned to establishing equality between men and women. The government has tried to do this by giving both sexes economic independence. Steps have been taken to make it easier for women to combine having a family and a job.

Women make up more than half the population, and comprise about 50% of the labor force. Most women work in Sweden; it is rare to come across someone who does not have a job, whether part-time or full-time. Mothers taking care of their babies are usually on long maternity leave. It is not surprising that the rate of women working (82%) is the highest in Europe. One reason for this is because childcare amenities are both affordable and available. Thus, women continue working even after having children. The picture is not all rosy. Most women are still confined to certain occupations that are paid less than men. Nonetheless, the difference is small compared with other countries. Even as steps have been taken to give women more choices, they continue to be responsible for taking care of the children and doing the domestic chores.

INDEPENDENT ELDERLY

The extended family has lost its importance in Sweden because many people have moved from their hometowns to study and work in other parts of the country. So, for many of the elderly, family visits may occur only once a week on weekends if the family lives close by. For others, visits may be less frequent although contact is kept through other means.

In the welfare state the elderly are frequently cared for by the state rather than their relatives. Retirees are given pensions and housing allowances which ensure financial security and some independence.

Some of the elderly occupants of the many service apartments that are exclusively for the old.

More than 90% of those aged 65 and above live in ordinary homes, some modified to meet their needs. As most do not live with a younger relative, they receive help from home help services. These helpers do daily chores such as shopping, cleaning and cooking. Home visits by the district doctor and nurses are also made when the elderly are ill and cannot move about. At the same time, many municipalities run centers to give old people the opportunity to meet others and socialize.

Old people who are fairly fit can choose to live in apartment buildings, called service houses, owned and managed by the municipality. They enjoy subsidized home help, as well as a restaurant and activity rooms within the building. Those who are less able to fend for themselves live in old-age homes where round the clock care is available. These homes, however, are being phased out as more state support is given for the old in their own residences.

RELIGION

RECORDS SHOW THAT Christianity came to Sweden as early as A.D. 829 when a French Benedictine monk by the name of Ansgar arrived at the trading center of Birka to spread the gospel.

CHRISTIANITY

Later, British and German missionaries came and worked among the Swedes, but it was not until the 11th century, when systematic evangelization took place, that the country became Christianized. The town of Uppsala was made the seat of the archbishop in 1164 and, eventually, the first Swedish archbishop was appointed.

THE REFORMATION

The country embraced Protestantism in the 16th century under the guidance of Gustav Vasa, who later became head of the Swedish state church. When the Reformation came, there was not an immediate break from past Catholic practices. After the break up of the Scandinavian union of Norway, Denmark and Sweden, Vasa wanted to take away the economic power of the Catholic Church in the country. Together with Laurentius Andreae, his chancellor, and Olaus Petri, he introduced the teachings of Reformation leaders like Martin Luther and Philipp Melanchthon, and Protestant revivals began.

Above: **A toy star by the window at Christmas.**

Opposite: **The Golden Dome Church.**

As a result of Pietism, education, social welfare and mission activities were started and carried out by Christians. As a result, during most of this century, the Church of Sweden has been active in the ecumenical movement, which promotes the unity and cooperation of Christians around the world.

BREAKAWAY In 1527, with the parliament's approval, Vasa declared the Church of Sweden independent of the Catholic Church and confiscated its property. Some Catholic priests left Sweden rather than accept Protestantism, but others stayed and, together with the people, gradually accepted it. In 1544, Sweden officially became a Lutheran nation.

Olaus Petri served Swedish Protestantism in many ways. He prepared the Swedish New Testament, a hymnbook, a church manual and liturgy for the people. But his most important contribution was helping his brother, Laurentius, and Laurentius Andreae translate the Bible into Swedish.

After some time, the Catholic Church attempted to regain power but failed. Under Gustav II Adolf, Lutheranism became so strong that it was never again threatened. However, in the 18th and 19th centuries, the Church was swept by the Pietism movement, where people preferred a deep, personal religious experience to religious formality and orthodoxy.

LUTHERANISM

The origins of the Lutheran Church go back to Martin Luther, the 16th-century Roman Catholic priest who objected to some Catholic practices and started the revolution known as the Protestant Reformation. Through his actions and writings, he ushered in not only Protestantism, but also a seedbed for economic, political and social thought.

Lutherans, like all Protestant denominations, believe in the divinity and humanity of Jesus Christ and in the Trinity of God. They also have two sacraments—baptism and the Lord's Supper. The basic unit of government in Lutheranism is the congregation. It is led by either a pastor or a lay person who is elected from the membership of a council, which is made up of a congregation's clergy and elected lay persons.

THE CHURCH OF SWEDEN TODAY The Church of Sweden is still the dominant faith with 92% of the population belonging to it. Part of the reason is probably because Swedish children automatically become members of the Church at birth if at least one parent is a member. Membership can be renounced by the parents on behalf of the child within six weeks of birth. Members are entitled to leave the church at any time on application.

A young woman dons the traditional headdress of candles in celebration of a festival.

In spite of the high church membership, Sweden is basically a secular state, and religion plays a minor role in the lives of most people. Only about 5% of the population attend church regularly. Christian customs, however, vary greatly in different parts of the country. There is more church attendance in the areas which had originally experienced different revival movements in the 19th century.

Nonetheless, Swedes in general do keep their Christian customs by marrying in church, baptizing and confirming their children, and burying their dead with the Church of Sweden. There is still a bond between the Church and the state and parliament that passes the laws. And until 1991, the Church was responsible for maintaining population records, which it had done since the 17th century. The ordination of women in the Church has taken place since 1958, unlike some denominations where it is still an issue.

Until the period of Enlightenment at the turn of the 18th century, all Swedes were expected to be a part of the Church of Sweden. But since 1781, when the Edict of Toleration was issued, other religious groups have been accepted. Full freedom was guaranteed by law only in 1952.

FREE CHURCHES

Several other Christian denominations have churches in Sweden besides the Lutheran Church. The largest is the Catholic Church, which has recently received a boost to its membership as a result of immigration from Catholic countries.

There are a few Protestant denominations besides the Church of Sweden. These are known as the "free churches." Among them are the Pentecostal churches.

The Pentecostal movement gained prominence in the early 20th century in the United States and has rapidly spread to all parts of the world. Pentecostal services are enthusiastic and rousing, with an emphasis on music and congregational participation. They are attractive to people who are interested in social reforms and an alternative to the orthodoxy of the Church of Sweden. At present, Swedish Pentecostal churches continue to swell in membership and make up the largest Protestant denomination aside from the Lutheran Church. It is also the fastest growing religious movement in the country. Another growing denomination is the Mission Covenant Church of Sweden.

Some of these churches were founded as a reaction to the rigidity of the Church of Sweden, while others were imported from other countries, especially English-speaking ones.

OTHER RELIGIONS

Close to half a million Moslems form the largest group of non-Christians. They are made up of immigrants from Turkey, the Middle East and North Africa. The next largest group are the Jews who have had congregations in Sweden for more than two centuries. There are also small numbers of Buddhists, Hindus and Jehovah's Witnesses.

LANGUAGE

THE EARLIEST SOURCES of the languages spoken in Sweden today are found in runic inscriptions all over Scandinavia. To date, about 3,500 runic inscriptions have been discovered. They are found on different types of articles, especially weapons and ornaments such as spear blades and brooches. But the most enduring have been the runestones—solid slabs of stone carved with runic inscriptions and ornamental designs.

Opposite: **A colorful runestone in Mariefred.**

STONES

The earliest stone dates back to A.D. 300. Little is known about the stones' origin but they were thought to be linked to magic and sorcery. The most common material for runes was believed to be wood, but none of these have been preserved. The stones showed that there were two systems of alphabet: the older system with 24 letters, used from the 3rd to the 9th century, and the later one with 16 letters, simplifying the earlier one. The golden age of runic writing was in the 11th and 12th centuries, during which trade with the East was at its peak.

The runic symbols were usually set within a decorated snake or dragon coil, and sometimes included other ornamental designs. The stone cutter would occasionally embellish the commissioned text with additional information. It was from these stones that much was learned about the political, economic and cultural aspects of those times. These memorials also tell of the journeys of the Vikings—to as far as Byzantium and Baghdad—as they were erected in memory of someone who had died on such trips. From pictures on these stones, we learn of old Nordic sagas of the popular dragon slayer, Sigurd, and Thor, the thunder god.

The most famous stone is the 9th-century Rökstone in the province of Ostergötland, which is unique because it has no ornamental design and contains the longest runic text in the world.

GERMANIC LANGUAGE

Swedish is the main language in Sweden. It is the language of the government and business. Finnish is also spoken, but only by a small number of people, and usually by those living close to the Finnish border in the north. Lapp is spoken here too, especially among the older people. This is mainly confined to the Samis, the indigenous people of Sweden.

If you were to listen closely to Swedish, you would recognize some words. This is because English and Swedish belong to the same linguistic tree—Germanic—although they are of different branches. Primitive Norse, the root of Swedish, is the oldest of all Germanic languages. It belongs to the North Germanic branch while English, German and Dutch belong to the West Germanic branch.

The Swedish language, however, is not more than 1,000 years old. In the year 1000, one language, Primitive Norse, was still in use in the whole Scandinavian region. It evolved through the centuries, influenced by domestic changes as well as foreign impetus. Primitive Norse later developed into Rune Swedish which was the language used by the Vikings.

The alphabet that is now used, the Latin alphabet, was introduced in the 13th century through the spread of Christianity. The Swedish language then became more regulated and stable with the arrival of printing and the production of books in the 15th century.

Modern Swedish is usually dated from the year 1526, when a Swedish translation of the Bible's New Testament was first printed. Standard Swedish which emerged during the 17th century consists primarily of the Svea dialects spoken by the people around Stockholm.

Above: **A gathering of diners. Conversation flows freely in the huge banquet hall.**

Opposite: **Rock carvings reveal the languages of ancient Swedes.**

Opposite top: **A mother and her three children going through a book.**

Opposite bottom: **New technology, like this desktop design computer, has resulted in better books and newspapers for Sweden.**

MODERN SWEDISH

As contact with other cultures increased, more words were borrowed from other languages and became part of the Swedish language. This aspect of borrowing reflected the nature of Sweden's relationships with other countries and cultures. For example, German trade and military terms were absorbed during the Hansa period, and even later during the Thirty Years' War when Sweden collaborated with the Germans.

Present-day Swedish was only widely spoken from this century onward. A standard language, instead of dialects, was used increasingly for several reasons. A central administration, increased cultural interests, better means of communication and transportation all led to people using a more uniform language. Just as important were schools in which standard Swedish was taught.

At the same time, people were leaving the countryside for towns to work in industry. For many, leaving the rural districts also meant leaving behind their dialects. Standard Swedish began in the towns and spread easily to these rural, less densely populated areas.

In recent times, radio and television played significant roles in spreading a uniform language. Today, the media is still important in language learning. Many words continue to be borrowed from other languages, mainly from British and Americanized English. Words like jeans and ketchup have become part of the Swedish language. The Swedish language also borrowed many words from German.

The characteristic of the Swedish language, like other Scandinavian languages, is enclitic definite articles—the placement of the definite article ("the") after the noun (e.g., "person the"). Nouns take only one ending: the possessive "s." It has a tone or pitched accent, much like a singsong rhythm.

REGIONAL DIALECTS

There are several regional dialects but these are no longer widely spoken. They are grouped into six regions: the Svea dialects which are spoken in the provinces in the middle of the country; the Göta and South Swedish dialects used in the south; the Norrländ dialects spoken in the north; the Gotländ dialects spoken on the island of Gotländ; and the East Swedish dialects which include those spoken in Finland and in the Baltic state of Estonia.

Older people, especially those living in geographically isolated places such as the north, continue to use the dialect of their area.

Most young people speak standard Swedish but with a noticeable regional accent. These accents are so marked that Swedes are able to identify the regional origin of the speaker.

In many countries, the standard or national language comes from one dialect. This is true of Sweden as standard Swedish has it roots from the dialect spoken in the Mälar province where the capital, Stockholm, is found. Historically, this province has been the center of power and economic activity.

However, standard Swedish has developed on its own since it was widely spoken. It has adopted

words from other Swedish dialects and foreign languages, and evolved its own expressions.

ARTS

SWEDES ENJOY a diverse and developed cultural life, ranging from classical expressions such as opera and drama to more popular forms like the cinema and folk music. The official policy is that cultural attractions should be enjoyed by everyone, not just an elite who can afford it.

CULTURE FOR THE PEOPLE

Cultural events are accessible to everybody either through relatively low ticket prices for performances or the easy availability of facilities. This has been possible through state support, which ranges from subsidies for cultural groups to book publishing and film production.

Cultural habits have changed over the last decade with more and more people preferring popular cultural attractions instead of the traditional forms. Thus pop and rock music, the cinema and television win more followers than opera and drama, in spite of the presence of more theaters and performances than ever before. Swedes, however, have been careful to preserve their heritage and many visit museums and heritage centers around the country. There are some 300 institutions, including national museums of art, natural history, archeology and cultural history; county and municipal museums which conserve the region's cultural heritage; and folk and specialized museums which are local in their focus.

Above: **A woodcarver carving another piece of art.**

Opposite: **A statue overlooking the sea, crowned with a halo by the sun.**

THE SOUND OF MUSIC

Music is the most important art form among the young, who love to listen to it or make their own. They are given the opportunity to learn to play different types of instruments in school where music is part of the curriculum.

The whole range of Western music can be found in Sweden, from opera to punk rock. Thus, there is no homogeneous style of music but rather many different kinds such as classical music, folk music, pop and opera. Although some of this music has been imported from other countries, or has been influenced by foreign music, there are still some types which are seen as being intrinsically Swedish, both by Swedes and by foreigners.

FOLK MUSIC Originating in peasant society in the 18th and 19th centuries, folk music is still sung and greatly enjoyed today. In the 1960s, efforts were made by experts and institutions to preserve this musical heritage which had been overshadowed by popular music. The traditions in and enthusiasm for folk music are kept alive through clubs, fiddlers' guilds, teachings and competitions. Annual festivals, such as the Music on Lake Siljian Festival for fiddlers, attract many participants and large audiences.

Originally, folk songs were sung at work and at play without instrumental accompaniment. The long, cold northern winter nights gave rise to many songs which were sung while chores such as spinning, repairing and tool-making were carried out. These songs took many forms: some were long ballads telling a story while others were humorous ones. Religious songs were also sung.

Many songs were first learned from books and later passed on orally. Today, some of these are still passed on in the same way as Swedes are fond of singing and dancing when they gather for traditional festivals, such as during Midsummer. Singing games, in which the lyrics are acted out, are especially popular with children who learn them from an early age.

It was only in the last century that instruments like the fiddle and accordion were used to accompany songs. This tradition began when the violin became a popular instrument in the countryside. The fiddler has occupied a special place in Swedish folk music history. During the 18th century and early part of the 19th century, fiddlers were much sought after to provide the music for weddings and dances. Local melodies were handed down from one fiddler to another.

At the same time, the fiddler was looked upon as a magical figure, involved in sorcery and superstition. Stories abound about magic fiddles and fiddlers who were taught to play by Näcken, a diabolical water spirit. In the later part of the 19th century, fiddlers were avoided when people associated them with the devil.

THE BALLAD TRADITION This is another heritage which is still enjoyed. Most, if not all, Swedes look to Carl Michael Bellman, an 18th century poet and musician, as the father of the Swedish ballad. His songs, which reflected life on the streets and in the taverns of his time, are still sung. A Bellman festival is held every year in Stockholm.

It was, however, modern troubadour Evert Taube who helped sustain the present interest in ballads. He was not just a balladeer but also a visual artist and prose writer who captured the popular imagination. He has been, and is still often thought of as, the "national poet." His themes center around the sea, the Swedish nature and South America, where he spent some time in his youth.

Carl Michael Bellman's popular drinking songs and parodies in the 1760s consisted of borrowed music from the works of others, with the tunes revised when necessary. He would then perform them to his own accompaniment on his zither.

Some Swedish organizations have established 240 people's parks, a type of outdoor entertainment hall for dancing, theater shows and summer concerts. These people's parks are partly financed by the government.

SAMI MUSIC The music of the Samis, believed to be the oldest form of music in Europe, reflects their nomadic history and way of life. It is very different from Swedish and other European music. For example, the *jojk* is a spontaneous, improvised song which recalls people or places and invokes emotions linked to that memory. It is intensely personal and sung without accompanying instruments. Musical instruments are rarely used in Sami music.

MUSICAL INSTRUMENTS The revival of folk music resulted in renewed interest and enthusiasm for folk music instruments. The interest has been so great that there are now courses in making and playing them.

Instruments with drones—which make low-pitched sounds—are especially popular. These include the bowed harp, bagpipes, the hurdy-gurdy, the Swedish zither, the jew's harp, and older types of keyed fiddles such as the silver drone-keyed fiddle and contradrone double-keyed fiddle.

The fiddle was the main instrument of folk music for several centuries until the mid-19th century when the accordion became popular. One type of fiddle found only in Sweden is the keyed fiddle, which continues to be popular today both in terms of playing and making it. This instrument is played with a bow and the strings are stopped by keys instead of fingers. It is fitted with drone strings which give a characteristic tonal sound.

Old wind instruments like the wooden flute and the clarinet are still used while those like the cow horn and the *lur,* a type of wooden trumpet, are used for herding cattle. Herding music—calls and signals used for communicating with the animals—is thought to be Sweden's oldest surviving domestic musical tradition.

ART

It is always a pleasure to go for a walk in a city or town as one might come upon a painting or a whimsical sculpture around a corner. Art in Sweden is part of everyday life, not just a collection of important paintings housed in a museum. Modern Swedish artists enjoy strong followings while aspiring painters and sculptors receive training at all levels, from study circles to colleges.

Sweden has its share of internationally well-known painters, such as turn-of-the-century artists Carl Larsson and Anders Zorn. The most well-known of Sweden's sculptors is Carl Milles, who was very successful in the United States where he worked for several years. There is a major work by Milles in almost every large town in Sweden.

Swedish artists have been greatly influenced by art on the European continent. But modern artists have also developed their own ideas and created certain recognizable Swedish styles.

Perhaps the best example of art as a daily affair is found in Stockholm's subway network. Dubbed the world's longest art gallery, half of the capital's 99 subway stations have been decorated with paintings, sculptures, engravings and mosaics. More than 70 artists have contributed to the throbbing and colorful work which makes catching the train such a pleasure.

The gallery was started in the late 1940s when the subway system was first built. There are different works of art that depict and reflect the spirit of each decade. There is something for every taste in this art gallery: a 60-foot human profile in terazzo; tiles and cobblestones; platform pillars that have been turned into giant trees; fantasy beetles in glass cases; and even a 315-foot long photo montage of present-day Sweden.

Top: **A work by painter Carl Larsson.**

Bottom: **A worker dipping toy horses in red paint.**

THE GLASSBLOWER'S MAGIC

Glass-making in Sweden, which began in the 16th century, is as much an industry as it is an art form. Most of the glassworks are found in the region of Smaland in the south.

Here, master glassblowers work with designers to create "glass art" which is either unique or limited in number. Many Swedes collect glass pieces like people do paintings, and the designs of certain artists are much sought after. Glassblowers also use skills passed on for centuries to produce items for daily use.

Some of the glassworks have revived a local tradition, known as *hyttsill*. It recalls the days when these glassworks were also meeting places where villagers gathered around the furnaces to gossip and bake herring and potatoes, to the accompaniment of music by a fiddler or an accordionist.

THEATER

The roots of modern Swedish theater are found in the 18th century when King Gustav III opened the doors of his theater to the commoners. Prior to that, court theaters were opened only to the aristocracy. In those days, the actors spoke Swedish instead of French, as in the rest of Europe.

Today, a wide range of work is staged in the country's many theaters. Classical, modern, experimental and children's plays find their place in the cultural scene. There are two national theaters in Stockholm: the Opera and the Royal Dramatic Theater, both of which were built by Gustav III.

There are, however, municipal theaters in other parts of the country which cater to the population outside the capital. The idea of folk theater (theater for everyone) gave rise to the touring drama company which helped popularize this art form in the whole of Sweden.

Ingmar Bergman first achieved international fame with his 1956 film, The Seventh Seal. *This was followed by more outstanding Oscar-winning pictures like* Wild Strawberries, Through a Glass Darkly, Cries and Whispers, *and* Fanny and Alexander.

MOVIES

Swedes go to an average of two movies a year, and usually to an American one. Only a small percentage go to Swedish movies, as most of these are not of high quality.

The Swedish Film Institute was set up in 1963 to ensure that Swedish movies would continue to be made. About 20 to 25 Swedish movies are made each year, all of which are financed by the institute. In turn, the institute receives money from a percentage of sales of movie tickets and video rentals. The movies made range from thrillers to comedies to art films. In general, Swedish directors do not make light-hearted movies. Instead, many concentrate on political and social issues or on the problems of the people.

While most Swedish movies are shown only in Sweden, there have been a few which were box office hits in other countries. Today, the name of Ingmar Bergman is synonymous with outstanding movies, especially abroad. He is still popular even though he has left movie production and returned to the theater where he started his brilliant career.

Bergman, who has been called one of the greatest movie directors by the Hollywood community, made many classics which reflected his view of his compatriots and country. In his earlier films, his stark and intense images, often filmed on a rugged island in the Baltic Sea, opened for audiences around the world a window on the soul of the modern-day Viking.

Like other areas of Swedish art and culture, there is a special movie niche for children. Much attention is paid to producing movies for them, both animated and non-animated. Many of these are based on much-loved children's stories and well-known characters like Pippi Longstocking.

ALFRED NOBEL AND THE NOBEL PRIZES

Every year on December 10, Nobel prizes—the world's most prestigious—are given away in a glittering ceremony by the king of Sweden. These prizes are the legacy of Swedish inventor and industrialist Alfred Nobel, who in his will stipulated that they should be given to those who have "conferred the greatest benefit on mankind."

The prizes, reflecting Nobel's interests, were originally given in five areas: physics, chemistry, physiology or medicine, literature and peace. An economics award was added in 1968 in his memory. The Peace Prize is awarded by a committee in Norway while the rest are given by Swedish institutions in Stockholm.

Nobel is perhaps less well-known as the inventor of dynamite and as a shrewd entrepreneur who founded some 90 factories and companies all over the world. He patented 355 of his inventions, of which explosives were the most famous.

AUGUST STRINDBERG TO ASTRID LINDGREN

The greatest Swedish writer in the 20th century is Pär Lagerkvist, who won a Nobel Prize in 1951. His writings during the 1920s included an autobiographical novel and love poetry, but his best works involved a search for vital, often religious, values.

Sweden has a long literary tradition which began in the Middles Ages. Today, the more popular forms of Swedish literature for both writers and readers are the novel and poetry.

Through history, Swedish literature has reflected the concerns of its time. In this century, for example, many books have been written by authors from working class backgrounds in defense of democracy, reflecting the country's development as a democratic and welfare state. In general, today's writers are more concerned with global issues such as the environment, and are moving away from the more provincial themes of earlier writers.

Literature is thriving in Sweden; there are many young, prolific authors who enjoy a following. However, a Swedish Author's Fund has been set up to provide a salary to a large number of established writers.

Quite a few Swedish writers have achieved international fame and had their works translated into other languages. Among the most well-known is August Strindberg, who wrote plays as well as novels. A brilliant writer, he breathed life into Swedish theater at the end of the 19th century. His plays—like his other works, usually critical of society—have been produced in many countries and some are still being performed all over the world.

One of the most famous authors in Swedish literary history is Selma Lagerlöf, who lived from 1858 to 1940. She won the Nobel Prize for literature in 1909. While her works were mainly based on Sweden, her creative fantasy had an appeal beyond the country's borders. She wove elements of the supernatural, influenced by folk tales and legends, into her stories about the countryside.

The work that brought her the most fame was a children's book which

has become a classic. Called *The Wonderful Adventures of Nils*, this book started as a geographical reader for schoolchildren but became so popular that it has been translated into more than 40 languages.

A more familiar name today is Astrid Lindgren, who has written many books for children. One of the characters she created in 1945, Pippi Longstocking, remains a much-read and well-loved figure in Sweden and elsewhere. Lindgren mixes fantasy with reality and creates mischievous characters that appeal greatly to children.

Lindgren did much to raise the standards of Swedish literature; she occupies a special place in the country's literary tradition. In addition to Lindgren, there are other writers of children's books which enjoy immense readership because they cater to the needs of children rather than adults.

Swedish literature for children is world famous.

LEISURE

IN GENERAL, Swedes spend a lot of time pursuing leisure activities as the working population enjoys six to 10 weeks of vacation a year. Traditionally, July is the month in which the country all but stops as most people take their summer vacations.

Most leisure activities involve the outdoors as Swedes enjoy being close to nature in order to escape city life as much as possible. These pursuits enable them to combine their two great interests—being with their families and being in the countryside.

Playing some kind of sport is the number one pastime. Sports are taken seriously, whether played competitively or just for fun.

Opposite: **A Tall Ship Race in Stockholm.**

Left: **Picking whortle-berries, a favorite leisure activity with Swedes of all ages.**

SPORTS

The success of Swedish tennis players on the world scene in the past 20 years has done much to promote the game in Sweden. Superstars such as Stefan Edberg, Mats Wilander and the legendary Bjorn Borg have helped put Sweden on the world sports map. But tennis is only one of many competitive sports in which Swedes excel.

Almost as popular as tennis is ice hockey, both as a game and as a spectator sport. Sweden is one of the top five ice hockey nations in the world, and always one of the favorites in world championship games.

Tennis champion Stefan Edberg in action. Edberg first made a name for himself by winning the 1985 Australian Open. Since then, he has added the U.S. Open and Wimbledon titles to his collection.

Swedes have also distinguished themselves in the prestigious Canada Cup competition against powerful teams like Canada and the Soviet Union. Swedish players like Mats Naslund have made a name for themselves and won championship medals while playing in the North American National Hockey League.

Needless to say, Swedes dominate winter sports like alpine skiing, but they also excel in soccer and table tennis. In spite of having such a small population, Sweden has done very well internationally. Part of this is due to the fact that sports are encouraged at an early age, and there are training programs and facilities to sustain and develop children's interests.

Children also attend "sports high schools," where academic work is combined with training. There are now more than 60 such schools which are subsidized by the state.

Dad and Mom watch as a little boy makes his big splash in the water.

STARTING YOUNG

Many children, looking to sports stars such as Borg, Naslund and Edberg as role models, are anxious to participate in competitive sports even before their teens. In fact, many of today's sports stars started when they were young.

Junior competitions like the Donald Duck Cup—the biggest tennis tournament for children in the 11–15 year age group—do much to spur young hopefuls to train and to give them a taste of competition.

Like other aspects of Swedish society, the sports movement is very well organized. It is able to provide the necessary coaching and systematic training for the thousands of young people who are a part of it. Another reason youth activities are so well-developed is because of the large number of unpaid coaches—nearly half a million—who dedicate themselves to training children.

Sports are compulsory in schools, and this, together with the many sports clubs and organizations, ensures that young talent is developed.

An endless army of cross-country skiers in the Vasa Race.

MASS SPORTS

Swedes enjoy doing things collectively and this is true in sports. Mass races, where the participants number in the thousands, are a very old tradition.

Often, mass events involve long distances, allowing participants to test their endurance. There are several mass sports events throughout the year which attract people like bees to honey.

The most famous is the Vasa Race for cross-country skiers, who compete in a grueling 55-mile race from Salen to Mora in the province of Dalarna. Held the first Sunday in March, it commemorates the escape of Gustav Vasa from the 1521 "Bloodbath of Stockholm." This popular race attracts more than the 12,000 allowed to participate every year.

Other popular events that are incentives to keep fit are the 18-mile Lidingö Race for joggers; the two-mile Vansbro Swim; and the 180-mile

EVERYMAN'S RIGHT

There is one right which everyone, young and old alike, respects in Sweden. This is the "Everyman's Right" or *Allemansrätt* ("AHL-ler-mahns-RAT"), an ancient tradition which is not written in law. It allows anyone to use any wood or field, regardless of ownership. It is therefore possible to walk and gather wild flowers and mushrooms, or even camp, on private property. There are no laws of trespass. This right, which the people treasure, is rarely abused. Those who make use of it are careful not to destroy the nature that they have come to appreciate.

Vättern Circuit, a two-day bicycle race.

Another mass event is the O-ringen, a five-day orienteering race which attracts as many as 20,000 people who run cross-country using a compass and a map for direction.

Fishing is perhaps the most popular non-competitive sport for Swedes. Given the numerous lakes, rivers and streams that hold countless salmon, perch and pike, it is hardly surprising that some 1 million people indulge in this pastime.

This is Sweden: the people do not go into the woods to get away from the hustle and bustle of everyday life; rather they go into it to build a more private society together in the middle of nowhere.

LEARNING ABOUT NATURE

As most recreational activities in Sweden take advantage of the fresh air and rich natural landscape, children learn at an early age to appreciate their environment. As more than half of the Swedish land mass is wooded, there are plenty of opportunities for nature treks and learning first-hand about the country's flora and fauna.

A special feature in school programs is the frequent use of field trips to supplement classroom learning. Many of these trips teach students about ecology and the natural environment.

Not surprisingly, walking is a popular pastime, and families often go off on long treks together during the warmer months. These walks usually turn into nature studies as children are taught to identify different types of wild flowers, trees and birds. There is also a chance of spotting an elk, a bear or even a lynx.

There is a network of marked trails all over the country. Many of these are dotted with rest stations which allow trekkers to spend the night in some comfort. The most well-known trail is the Kungsleden (Royal Route) in the north which is more than 300 miles long.

Cross-country skiing replaces walking in the winter. This form of skiing is almost second nature to Swedes, although the young of today prefer the thrill of downhill skiing.

IT'S SUMMERTIME

Summer in Sweden is short and hectic. From the very start of the season, Swedes grab their vacation bags, pack into cars, buses and trains, and head out to the countryside or onto the beaches.

Most families have a summer house in the countryside or have access

A summer house in the province of Södermanland.

to one where they spend a good part of their vacations. Typically, many days are spent picking different types of wild berries like cloudberries, wild strawberries, raspberries and blueberries. Toward autumn, the hunt is on for that very Swedish fruit, the lingenberry, as well as rose hips and blackberries.

The end of summer also signals the time for picking mushrooms. Walks in the woods turn into mushroom hunting expeditions. Young and old search intensely in the undergrowth for chanterelles, cepes, ringed boletuses and other edible fungi.

Berry and mushroom picking is taken so seriously here that there are not only organized trips to the woods during the season but also classes that teach about different kinds of fungi, especially which are edible and which are not.

Sailors preparing the sail for another round of the Tall Ship Race.

DIET AND EXERCISE

Sports bodies and organizations promoting outdoor activities have long campaigned for healthy living and eating habits among Swedes. Their efforts culminated in a national campaign, the "Diet and Exercise Campaign," launched by the National Board of Health and Welfare.

The message of this 10-year campaign, which ended in 1981, was exercise regularly, have better eating habits (by consuming less fat and sugar), and do not smoke or drink.

While this message, based on recommendations by a group of medical experts, was aimed at the individual, the ways in which the National Board of Health and Welfare would fulfill the objectives were through organizations. Part of the campaign was thus directed at companies and

Swedes take to the sea in their motorboat.

local authorities. The result was the building of physical welfare centers aimed at encouraging the middle-aged and elderly toward better living habits. Companies also appointed physical welfare advisers and developed occupational health services. At the same time, the National Board of Health and Welfare and county councils provided a wide range of health education programs, from anti-drug to dieting.

The campaign has been successful perhaps only in instilling a consciousness in Swedes for a healthy lifestyle. While many profess an interest in their physical well-being, surveys show that only 25% of the population exercise regularly. This despite the fact that the country is capable of accommodating a wide variety of healthy activities that one can take part in—from hiking to skiing to water sports of all sorts.

FESTIVALS

MANY OF THE FESTIVALS IN SWEDEN can be attributed to the country's climate, geography and history. Given the extreme contrasts in weather conditions in different parts of the country (due to its length and northerly position), it is not surprising that the transition from one season to the next is marked by some kind of celebration.

Although many modern Swedes are quite secular in their thinking—and there is a decline in church attendance and participation in religious activities—religious holidays are still the main features on their festive calendar and religious traditions continue to prevail.

Opposite: **Children at a farm picking flowers to make garlands for the Mid-summer festivals.**

Below: **Two children looking at the candles on the Christmas tree.**

LENT

Shrove Tuesday, the day before Lent, is still celebrated although mostly in a secular way, with people in the north eating a hearty meat stew and those in the south enjoying *semla* rolls stuffed with almond paste and whipped cream.

Swedes no longer fast during Lent, not since the Protestant Reformation in the 16th century when Sweden became a Lutheran state.

Many do, however, practice a custom that has a symbolic association

with Christ's suffering on his way to his crucifixion at Golgotha. This involves gathering bare twigs and branches of the birch tree and decorating them with brightly colored feathers. These branches gradually sprout leaves after being placed in a vase of water.

The Feast of Valborg begins with a breakfast of pickled herring and a strong drink. Later in the day, it ends with the lighting of bonfires which can be seen for miles at night.

EASTER

Easter week, which starts with Palm Sunday, is still solemnly observed. There are no palm processions as in Catholic countries, perhaps because no palms can grow in Sweden's cold climate. Instead, the people bring early budding varieties of willow branches back to their homes and their offices so that they sprout leaves on Palm Sunday. In some parts of the country, these branches are called "palms."

The lighter side of Easter is found in the dressing up of children as "Easter hags" on Maundy Thursday, or the eve of Good Friday. The children visit their neighbors, leaving a small decorated card and hoping in return for sweets or a coin.

In western Sweden, this Easter card or letter, as it is known, is often slipped unseen into a mailbox or under the door with the identity of the sender kept secret.

Also in this part of the country, it is common to have a huge bonfire with villages competing to see which can make the biggest. Fireworks are also let off as part of the festivities. These customs stem from the superstitious belief in the past that witches were out and about practicing their evil, particularly during Easter week.

It was thought that they flew on their broomsticks on Maundy Thursday to meet the devil and return the following Saturday. To protect themselves against the black magic whizzing around, people lit bonfires, shot their firearms into the sky and painted crosses on their doors.

THE FEAST OF VALBORG

The Feast of Valborg, also known as Walpurgis Night, takes place on April 30. It does not, however, involve a feast of food but rather one of

song. This is the evening in which the people welcome spring, although in the north it is still weeks away.

This festival is especially celebrated by university students who gather in the thousands at the country's oldest university at Uppsala. Here, wearing white caps to mark the change in seasons, they sing school songs and traditional odes to spring.

This is followed by parties which last well into dawn of the next day, which is May Day. Meanwhile, the rest of the population gathers around community bonfires to make speeches and sing a welcome to the return of light.

May Day sees the start of springtime activities like picnics and outdoor games. It is also marked by parades and speeches by labor and political leaders as it is Labor Day as well.

A large crowd gathers by a seaside bonfire to celebrate the Feast of Valborg.

Marching bands parade down the streets of Stockholm.

LET'S CELEBRATE!

NATIONAL DAY This day, on June 6, is a low-key affair in contrast to other countries which celebrate their national days with pomp and ceremony. It is celebrated in schools and most towns with parades and speeches. However, it is a normal working day and that perhaps has added to the ordinariness of the commemorations.

MIDSUMMER There is much festivity during Midsummer, traditionally celebrated on June 23. Now it is celebrated on the Friday closest to this day. This is the time when summer days are at their longest, and the midnight sun is making its much awaited appearance.

On this day, people gather garlands of flowers and leafy branches and decorate homes, cars, churches and other public places with them. Then they proceed to gather around a maypole to dress it with flowers and leaves. This tall, floral-bedecked cross is erected in the village square or a playground and the dancing begins. Young and old ring the maypole dancing and singing. Some places, like Dalarna in central Sweden, are famous for their Midsummer activities and attract hordes of tourists.

As in most traditional holidays, there are superstitions attached. It was believed that the dew on that night held special properties, and if collected, could be used to cure illnesses. Certain plants were also collected for the same purpose. Those who were single would dream of whom they would marry if they picked a bouquet of seven or nine types of flowers and placed them under their pillow. The future could also be seen by eating "dream herring" and "dream porridge" with plenty of salt in it.

Family and friends hold hands and go around the maypole singing and dancing during Midsummer festivities.

NEW YEAR'S EVE This is an anti-climax after the Christmas activities. Many spend New Year's Eve quietly at home with family or friends. There is no celebration in the streets, although people do let off fireworks.

CALENDAR OF FESTIVALS

Jan 1	New Year's Day	June 23	Midsummer
Jan 6	Twelfth Night	Oct/Nov	All Saint's Day
Mar/Apr	Easter	Nov 11	St. Martin's Day
April 30	Feast of Valborg	Dec	Beginning of Advent
May 1	May Day	Dec 24	Christmas Eve
June 3	Ascension	Dec 25	Christmas Day
June 6	National Day	Dec 31	New Year's Eve

CHRISTMAS

The festival that Swedes look forward to the most is Christmas. Almost the whole of December is spent in preparation and anticipation of Christmas Eve, the climax of all the festivities. Early December signals the start of celebrations with many going to church. Wreaths, lights and Christmas trees pop up all along streets and town squares on the first Sunday.

At home, the first of four candles for each of the four Sundays leading up to Christmas is lit on special candlesticks for the occasion. Children open the first window of their Advent calendars, which are actually cards with windows to open for each day until Christmas. Many also hang a lighted star, made of straw, paper or metal, at their windows.

Next is Lucia on December 13. This has little to do with the original dedication of the day to St. Lucia of Syracuse. This occasion was earlier celebrated with plenty of food and drink because it was the longest night of the year according to folk tradition, and both people and animals needed extra nourishment.

Santa Claus (also known as the Christmas gnome in Sweden) and his assistant about to visit yet another home to bring gifts and laughter.

The present Lucia celebrations can be traced back to a mixture of historical and popular practices. In many homes, the morning begins with a daughter of the family acting as St. Lucia, dressed in a long white gown and wearing a crown of candles, bearing a tray of coffee, saffron buns, ginger snaps and sometimes spicy mulled wine.

In schools, clubs and community gatherings, a St. Lucia is chosen from among the girls. She will lead a train of attendants clad in white gowns—girls with glitter in their hair and boys wearing tall, conical hats and bearing a star on a stake. They sing traditional carols and songs.

Many offices and public organizations give Lucia parties and guests help themselves to the traditional fare after the singing by a Lucia procession.

The climax is of course Christmas Eve. Many start the day by decorating the Christmas tree with typically Swedish ornaments: the Christmas gnome, the Noel goat, ginger cookies in different shapes.

At about 3 p.m., the feasting begins and continues into the evening. The family spends days preparing for the traditional *smörgåsbord*. The children wait in anticipation after the meal as the Christmas gnome, a sort of Santa Claus, is expected to appear. They believe that he lives under the floorboards of the house or barn and spends the year looking after the family.

The traditional wrapping of Christmas presents is taught by Mom.

It is customary for someone to be disguised as this spry old gent and make a visit for the benefit of the young members of the family. It is a visit mixed with trepidation and excitement for the little ones as they have to invite him to have a meal of rice porridge (said to be his favorite food).

Church services celebrating Christmas are held in the morning. Aside from that, the rest of the day is spent quietly with family. Some families continue the merrymaking on Twelfth Night or Epiphany which falls on January 6. It all comes to an end a week later on Knut's Day when the Christmas tree is taken down, but not before there is a party for the children and their friends who help dismantle the tree by eating the edible goodies. Then they throw the tree out with a traditional song.

FOOD

FOODS COMMONLY FOUND in other northern European countries and the United States are also available in Sweden. These include familiar items like beef, pork, poultry, dairy products, potatoes, tomatoes, carrots, oranges, apples and berries.

FOOD AVAILABLE

The daily diet of a Swede is made up of meat or fish, vegetables and potatoes, a *smörgås* (an open-faced sandwich) or two, cheese, a bowl of yogurt, and milk, which accompanies most meals. Swedes are also great coffee drinkers and the coffee break is virtually a national institution.

Although only a small proportion of national resources are used in farming, the country is totally self-sufficient in agriculture. Food prices are thus higher here than in most other European countries partly because of Sweden's protective measures against foreign products. The large share of domestic production also means that few foreign or exotic foods have become common features on the family table. This is slowly changing as the population becomes less homogeneous. Also, foods characteristic of the immigrants are influencing what the Swedes now eat. Nonetheless, there are certain foods which can be distinguished from others as Swedish cuisine. While beef and pork are the preferred meats, it is not unusual to find reindeer and elk meat on some dinner tables. Another little-known food item is the cloudberry, a tiny gold-colored fruit which grows in the north and is a favorite of many.

Fish is a firm favorite, the two most common types being salmon and herring. A "typical" Swedish meal would not be complete without one or both of these fish, usually prepared in a variety of ways.

Above: **A father and son having a chat while fishing.**

Opposite: **Christmas food galore! A table is loaded with delicious Swedish food that will make anyone who sees it hungry.**

SEASONAL FOOD

Where the seasons bring changes in the style of living, the food consumed changes with the climate too. Spring means the end of a long winter, and with it comes Easter food, including eggs done in different ways, leg of lamb, and *semla*—a roll normally eaten before Lent. This roll, made from wheat flour, is filled with marzipan and whipped cream and usually eaten with a bowl of hot milk and cinnamon.

More cold foods are eaten in the summer, with some people having only a bowl of fermented milk for dinner. Potatoes, together with *matjessil* ("MAHT-che-sill") or sweet pickled herring, sour cream and chopped chives, form part of the traditional midsummer day's lunch.

All kinds of berries, from wild strawberries to cloudberries, are picked and consumed in large quantities in the summer. A typical Swedish berry is the *lingon* or cowberry, a red bittersweet fruit which is usually made into jam. This jam is the Swedish equivalent of tomato ketchup; young and old alike eat it with everything, from pancakes to meatballs.

Berry picking continues into the autumn, which is also the season for picking (and eating) wild mushrooms. A popular mushroom is the gold-colored chantarelle, which can be bought

An egg packing plant in the region of Västergötland.

in stores but is very expensive. This is also the time for eating shellfish, especially crayfish.

Hot, robust meals like stews are preferred in winter. A heavy pea soup with salted pork is traditionally served on Thursdays at this time of the year. This meal is eaten with pancakes and jam. Other popular dishes include stewed brown beans with fried pork, and beef stew served with *lingon* jam, pickled beetroot and cucumber.

TABLE MANNERS

Swedes, in general, like things well-ordered. This is true even in social entertainment where rules of behavior are followed. These rules apply to formal dinners as well as casual meals. For example, Swedes are always punctual because it is considered bad manners to be late. Many arrive early and wait to present themselves at the door at the appointed time. It is customary to bring a gift for the hostess, perhaps a box of chocolates or even a bouquet of flowers.

To start the meal, the host gives a short speech and then raises his glass for the first *skål* ("skol"), or toast, to welcome his guests. The guests are expected to reply with the word *skål*, and then establish eye contact with fellow guests, especially those sitting across and immediately to the left and right. Eye contact is re-established after a sip is taken.

At a formal dinner, guests are not supposed to drink their wine unless in a *skål*. They either have to offer a toast or wait to be toasted. At an informal

Roast, anyone? A chef prepares some for his hungry diners.

meal, the host will usually announce that "drinking is free," which means that guests are allowed to drink without having to *skål* each other. A popular story explaining the origin of this custom tells of the Vikings who trusted no one. It was the practice to toast others while keeping an eye out for any unpleasant surprises (like a stab in the heart).

Toward the end of the meal, the guest on the left of the hostess is expected to give a short speech of thanks on behalf of the others. Children are taught at an early age to thank their hostess by saying, "*Tack för maten*," meaning "Thank you for the food." Guests are expected to telephone or write a note to thank the hostess the following day.

When cooking, Swedish cooks use margarine or butter instead of oil. Cream sauce and a jam made of wild berries often accompany roasted meats, especially game.

TRADITIONAL METHODS

The way in which a lot of Swedish food is prepared today is an inheritance of the past. A good example is found in the preparation of fish, which has long been a staple in the diet. The country's long coastline and numerous lakes have yielded a rich variety of species.

In the old days, the irregular supply of the main types of fish as well as the difficulty of fishing during winter in the frozen north gave rise to different methods of preserving fish. Therefore, it is not surprising to still find a number of dishes which include salted, dried or smoked fish.

Gravad lax ("GRAH-vahd lax"), or marinated salmon, must surely be one of the most well-known Swedish dishes. Its origins are ancient as *gravning*, or marinating, is one of the oldest curing methods. *Gravning* comes from the word *begrava*, which means bury. The original method was to bury the fish after salting it sparingly in order to preserve it because salt was an expensive commodity. This method of preparation also gave rise to fermentation, another old Swedish preservation method.

Nowadays, marinated fish is not buried, let alone fermented. Instead, the fish is rubbed with salt, sugar and herbs and left to cure for a day or two in the refrigerator.

Two varieties of fish still enjoyed by Swedes are salmon and herring. But yesterday's daily staples have become today's delicacies and these fish are usually part of an elaborate buffet. The Scandinavian salmon (different from its Pacific relative) was once so plentiful in and around Sweden that people working in salmon-rich areas had a clause written into their contracts to ensure that they would not have to eat this fish every day. Today, it is one of the most expensive fish in Sweden.

Meat was also dried and salted in the old days. *Spicken*, another word with ancient roots, used to refer to the method of stretching out meat and

fish on wooden sticks to dry in the sun, after which it would be salted. Today, while meats are still sun-dried and salted, fish is merely salted.

One area where tradition still prevails is in the baking of crispbread, sometimes called "hard bread." While most varieties of this unleavened, wholemeal rye bread are machine-made, some are still baked in old-fashioned wooden stoves in certain areas such as Dalarna in central Sweden. Originally, crispbread was coarse in texture, dry and durable due to the high temperature at which it was baked. This large, thin, round bread's peculiar characteristic was a hole in its center. A pole would be threaded through and it would be suspended from the ceiling above the family's wooden stove. That was the traditional method of storing crispbread in the country. Nowadays, it is possible to find a variety of crispbreads with different textures and hardness. Many still come with a hole in the center, but that is more for tradition.

THE SMORGASBORD

The best summary of Sweden's food heritage is found in the *smörgåsbord* ("SMOER-gos-bord"), which means "open sandwich table." Anyone taking this literally would be in for a surprise when confronted with the seemingly endless rows of dishes which make up this meal.

While the concept of this buffet-style meal is not uniquely Swedish, others do not match up to it because of its close association with old culinary traditions and its importance as the country's main cuisine.

The practice of laying out different dishes on the table is said to have started in the 16th century. The present form is a descendant of the *brännvin* table of the 18th century, which was the first course of a banquet laid on a separate table. Guests would enjoy this course—which consisted of *brännvin* (fiery wine), herring, anchovies, bread and strong cheese—while standing before taking their seats for the main meal.

Over the years, more dishes were

added to this first course until its peak in the 19th century when it began to be served both in homes and in restaurants. Today, the *smörgåsbord* is no longer the first course but the whole meal.

Modern Swedes do not have the time to prepare the enormous buffets of past centuries but instead offer scaled-down versions when entertaining at home. But on special occasions and especially at Christmas, they celebrate with a laden table which recalls their heritage.

There are five courses in the *smörgåsbord*, with several dishes making up each course. The first course consists of a variety of herrings (pickled, salted and marinated) and strong, hard cheeses accompanied by crispbread.

The second includes other fish dishes with salmon being the highlight. Cold meats make up the third that includes delicacies like dried leg of mutton and smoked reindeer. Salads and pickled vegetables are the usual accompaniments.

Among the warm, light dishes which make up the fourth are meatballs—every Swedish child's favorite—and Jansson's Temptation, a baked dish of potatoes and anchovies. The fifth is a fitting finale to this rich meal: creamy cakes, Swedish apple pies and an abundance of fresh fruits.

Above: **Swedish saffron buns.**

Opposite: **The longest *smörgåsbord* in the world, at Stockholm's King Street.**

CRAYFISH PARTY

This party is a uniquely Swedish celebration; one could almost say it is an invention. The season for eating crayfish starts August 8 when the law permits the catching and selling of these crustaceans. There were no traditions attached to crayfish consumption before the turn of the century. But with a fixed opening day to the season, Swedes have taken the opportunity to turn it into a celebration.

Groups of friends gather, usually on the evening of the 8th, to consume vast quantities of crayfish boiled in salted water and seasoned with flowering dill. The place is gaily decorated with lanterns, and everyone wears funny hats (such as paper crayfish with claws sticking out like horns) and paper bibs.

Only bread and a spiced cheese are eaten with this delicacy. All these are washed down by beer and, of course, *snaps*. One will hear the sounds of laughter and the singing of *snaps* songs well into the night during a crayfish party.

SNAPS

No *smörgåsbord* is considered complete without *snaps* ("snahps") or aquavit, which is always drunk by the glassful. Thankfully, *snaps* glasses are relatively small, but even a small quantity of *snaps* still packs a powerful punch. *Snaps* are made from potatoes or barley, and vary a great deal in flavor. Different types of herbs and spices, such as caraway seeds, cumin, and dill, are used in the flavoring. There are at least 20 flavored *snaps* to choose from.

The importance of *snaps* in Swedish drinking tradition is found in the drinking ritual. Noticeably there is no ritual to the drinking of beer, which is also drunk with the *smörgåsbord*. But for *snaps*, it is a must to raise glasses for a mutual toast before downing the aquavit, after which either the *skål* rule applies or guests are allowed to drink at their liberty.

But what Swedes really enjoy most is a song before gulping the *snaps*. These traditional drinking songs are sung by everyone and end almost in a shout. There are countless songs, some with witty lyrics and full of puns. Different occasions call for different songs, although they can be sung in any season. Some, such as those sung during Christmas, are learned from childhood.

FESTIVAL FOOD

For the most part of the year, Swedes go about the business of living with few festivals being celebrated. However, the most important date in their calendar is Christmas.

Early in December, the smell of spicy Christmas food being baked wafts through the air. Even those who rarely bake or have the time to do so (since most people work) will try their hand at turning out ginger snaps and saffron buns.

Semla rolls—filled with cream and marzipan—are favorite desserts during Lent.

Lucia Day on December 13 marks the start of festivities. In offices all around the country, people will gather in their coffee corners sipping spiced mulled wine and eating ginger snaps and saffron buns. The wine is a mixture of red and white aquavit, spiced with cinnamon, cloves and cardamom. This spicy, sweet brew is served piping hot with raisins and almonds in it.

Ginger snaps are popular, thin, crisp, spice cookies which are eaten year round. But it is still considered very much a part of Christmas baking. Children also have their share of the goodies, but for them hot chocolate will take the place of the hot wine.

The Christmas *smörgåsbord*, usually eaten in the afternoon of Christmas Eve, has certain dishes that are different from those found at buffets during the rest of the year. These include mustard-glazed baked ham, special sausages, pickled pigs' feet and sweet-sour red cabbage.

Certain dishes hark back to the days of old, such as "Dip in the Pot," which recalls the time when poor farm hands were invited to dip their bread in the broth in which ham and other meats had been boiled. That was the closest they got to tasting the ham. Today, a special herb-

flavored bread is used to dip in this tasty broth.

Another traditional dish is salted and dried stockfish. This dried fish is put into a solution of slaked lime on December 9, so that it will be sufficiently soaked when Christmas Day comes around. It is a dish which is either loved or hated because of its unusual flavor and smell.

Every young child in Sweden is told to leave a bowl of rice porridge for the Christmas gnome to eat when he comes to visit. This thick porridge is often eaten as a dessert on Christmas Eve. Rice is boiled with milk and cream, and served with sugar, cinnamon and a dot of butter to create this special porridge. Sometimes a single almond is added; it is believed that any single person who gets it in his or her portion will be married within the year.

In general, Christmas food is highly spiced, with cloves, ginger, allspice and bay leaves being the classic ingredients. To many Swedes, the spicy smells from the cooking and baking are as much a part of Christmas as the other rituals of this festival.

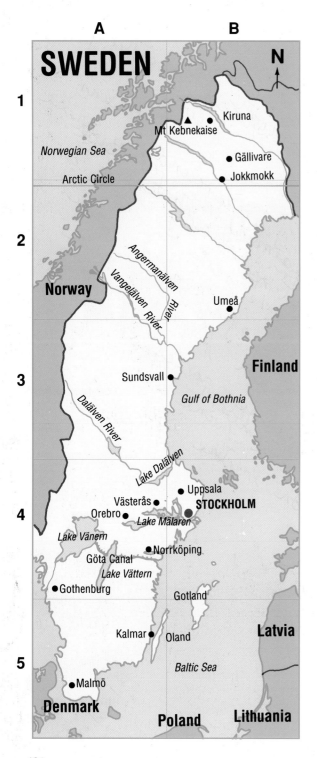

SWEDEN

N

A | B

1
Kiruna
Mt Kebnekaise
Gällivare
Jokkmokk

Norwegian Sea

Arctic Circle

2
Norway
Angermanälven River
Vangelälven River
Umeå

3
Sundsvall
Gulf of Bothnia
Dalälven River
Finland

Lake Dalälven
Uppsala
Västerås
STOCKHOLM
Orebro
Lake Mälaren
Lake Vänern
Norrköping
Göta Canal
Lake Vättern
Gothenburg
Gotland

4

Kalmar
Oland
Latvia

5
Baltic Sea
Malmö

Denmark
Poland
Lithuania

Angermanälven River A2	Latvia B5
Arctic Circle A2	Lithuania B5
Baltic Sea B5	Malmö A5
Dalälven River A4	Mount Kebnekaise B1
Denmark A5	Norrköping A4
Finland B3	Norway A2
	Norwegian Sea A1
Gällivare B1	Oland Island A5
Göta Canal A4	Orebro A4
Gothenburg A4	
Gotland Island B4	Poland B5
Gulf of Bothnia B3	
Jokkmokk B2	Stockholm B4
	Sundsvall B3
Kalmar A5	Umeå B2
Kiruna B1	Uppsala B4
Lake Dalälven A4	Vangelälven River A3
Lake Mälaren B4	Västerås A4
Lake Vänern A4	
Lake Vättern A4	

——— **International Boundary**
▲ **Mountain**
● **Capital**
● **City**
〜 **River**
Lake

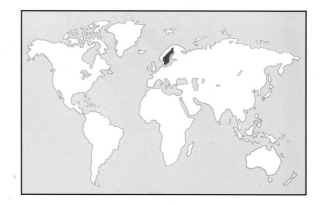

QUICK NOTES

LAND AREA
174,000 square miles

POPULATION
8.5 million

CAPITAL
Stockholm

PROVINCES
Blekinge, Bohuslan, Dalarna, Dalsland, Gotland, Gästrikland, Halland, Hälsingland, Härjedalen, Jämtland, Lappland, Medelpad, Norrbotten, Närke, Skåne, Småland, Södermanland, Uppland, Värmland, Västerbotten, Västergötland, Västmanland, Angermanland, Ostergötland

LONGEST RIVER
Dalälven (322 miles)

HIGHEST POINT
Kebnekaise (6,945 feet)

LARGEST LAKE
Vänern (2,156 square miles)

NATIONAL LANGUAGE
Swedish

MAJOR RELIGION
Christianity (Lutheran Church of Sweden)

CURRENCY
Krona (US$1 = 6.2 krona)

MAIN EXPORTS
Wood products, paper pulp and paper, cars, machinery, chemical products, iron ore and steel.

IMPORTANT ANNIVERSARIES
May Day (May 1)
National Day (June 6)

IMPORTANT LEADERS
Gustav Eriksson Vasa—instrumental in uniting the country in the 14th century. Led Sweden into Protestantism.

Gustav II Adolf—during his reign, Sweden became a European power in the 15th century. Killed in the Battle of Lützen after leading army to several successful victories in the Thirty Years' War.

Marcus Wallenburg—industrialist who was head of the Wallenburg family empire that owned a large part of the country's private industries.

Dag Hammarskjöld—Secretary-General of the United Nations. His strong leadership and organization in solving crises around the world gained him much respect. Killed in an air crash in 1961.

Olof Palme—Social Democrat prime minister, 1972–1976 and 1982–1986. Instrumental in putting country on international map. Assassinated in 1986.

GLOSSARY

Allemansrätt	Everyone's right to enter rural private property without permission.
gravad lax	Marinated salmon.
matjessil	Sweet pickled herring.
ombudsman	Official appointed to investigate complaints against public authorities.
samboende, sambo	A person one is living with.
semla	Wheat roll eaten during Lent.
skål	A toast (to one's health).
smörgås	Open-faced sandwich.
smörgåsbord	Buffet of Swedish specialties.
snaps	Aquavit.
spicken	Ancient method of stretching out meat and fish in the sun to dry.

BIBLIOGRAPHY

Hintz, Martin: *Enchantment of the World: Sweden*, Childrens Press, Chicago, 1985.
Knowlton, MaryLee (ed.): *Children of the World: Sweden*, Gareth Stevens Publishing, Milwaukee, 1987.
Larsson, Karl: *A Farm*, Putnam, New York, 1976.
Lindgren, Astrid: *Pippi Longstocking*, Viking, New York, 1983.

INDEX

PICTURE CREDITS
Life File Photo Library: 5 (two pictures),
30, 42, 45, 50, 51, 62, 70, 82, 108, 125
MacQuitty International Collection: 73,
122
Mark Markefelt: 8, 15, 17, 23 (bottom),
31, 35, 46 (bottom), 47, 63, 65, 76, 78,
95, 101, 114, 118, Back Cover
Svenskt Pressfoto: Front Cover, Title
Page, 4, 6, 7, 9, 10, 11, 12, 13, 14, 16,
23 (top), 27, 28, 29, 33, 36, 38, 39, 40,
41, 43, 46 (top), 48, 52, 53, 54, 55, 56,
58, 59, 60, 61, 66, 67, 68, 69, 71, 75,
79, 81 (two pictures), 83, 87 (two
pictures), 88, 89, 91, 93, 94, 96, 97, 98,
99, 102, 103, 104, 105, 107, 109, 110,
111, 112, 113, 115, 117, 119, 120, 123